# THE
# TIME-OUT
# SOLUTION

## A Parent's Guide for Handling Everyday Behavior Problems

### LYNN CLARK, Ph.D.

CB

CONTEMPORARY
BOOKS

CHICAGO · NEW YORK

**Library of Congress Cataloging-in-Publication Data**

Clark, Lynn. 1938–
The time-out solution : a parent's guide for handling
everyday behavior problems / Lynn Clark.
    p.  cm.
    Bibliography: p.
    Includes index.
    ISBN 0-8092-4522-1 : $7.95
    1. Discipline of children.   2. Timeout method.   3. Child
    rearing.   I. Title.
HQ770.4.C523   1989
649'.64—dc 19
                                        88-31772
                                             CIP

**Publisher's Note:**
  This book is designed to provide information on the
subject matter covered. It is sold with the understanding
that the publisher and author are not engaged in
rendering psychological, medical, or other professional
services.
  Rearing children is sometimes very difficult. If expert
assistance is needed, seek the services of a competent
professional. Appendix C describes ways to obtain
professional help.

Copyright © 1989 by Lynn Clark, Ph.D.
All rights reserved
Published by Contemporary Books, Inc.
180 North Michigan Avenue, Chicago, Illinois 60601
Manufactured in the United States of America
Library of Congress Catalog Card Number: 88-31772
International Standard Book Number: 0-8092-4522-1

Published simultaneously in Canada by Beaverbooks, Ltd.
195 Allstate Parkway, Valleywood Business Park
Markham, Ontario L3R 4T8 Canada

*To children*
*and those who rear them.*

# Contents

## PART I
## GOOD PARENTING BREEDS
## GOOD CHILDREN

Three child-rearing rules • Four common child-
rearing errors • Physical problems may contribute
to behavior problems • Reasons parents don't
discipline

Parents must agree on goals • Clear communications
between parent and child • How to give effective
commands • Children need discipline and lots of love

Actively ignore your child's bad behavior • Reward
good alternative behavior • Help your child practice
good behavior • Use Grandma's Rule • Set a good
example • Be an organized parent

## APPENDIXES
## MORE RESOURCES FOR
## HELPING YOUR CHILD

# Acknowledgments

I am especially indebted to Gerald Patterson, Rex Fore-hand, and their colleagues for much of this book's research and clinical foundations. Donald Baer introduced me to behavioral child management research when I was a graduate student at the University of Kansas. B. F. Skinner, for more than a half century, has contributed fundamental research on human behavior.

Gerald Patterson at the Oregon Social Learning Center and Mark Roberts at Idaho State University reviewed the manuscript, and their comments and recommendations improved the usefulness of *The Time-Out Solution*.

Carole Clark critiqued each of the many manuscript drafts and contributed true examples of problem behavior and parent-child interactions. Mary Ann Kearny and Virginia Lezhnev made suggestions regarding writing style and provided encouragement.

Individuals at Western Kentucky University who contributed to this book include Patrice Nolan, Lois Layne, Clinton Layne, Harry Robe, William Pfohl, Elsie Dotson, Ned Kearny, Fred Stickle, Livingston Alexander, Carl Martray, Delbert Hayden, and James Warwick. Many graduate and undergraduate students also contributed useful comments regarding the manuscript.

Copyediting was done by Beverly Cravens. Janet Allen helped type the manuscript revisions. Bettye Neblett offered valuable suggestions and provided swift, expert typing.

# Introduction

Six-year-old Jessica was out of control. When angry, she bit her wrist till it bled, screamed and swore, and hit her mother or attacked a wall or door in a fit of rage. Jessica *always* insisted on having her way. Once at a shopping center, she refused to accompany her parents back to their car. Instead, she forced them to chase her through parked cars and traffic. Severe scoldings and spankings were ineffective in stopping her from behaving like a brat. Jessica was in charge.

Early in my experience as a psychologist, I worked with Jessica and Mrs. Stiles, her mother. Mrs. Stiles agreed to try counseling, although she was pessimistic about changing her daughter. I didn't work directly with Jessica. Instead, I taught Mrs. Stiles effective methods of discipline and child management. She correctly applied these methods and, after a stormy eight weeks, Jessica's behavior changed dramatically. She didn't become an angel, but she became manageable.

During our counseling sessions, Mrs. Stiles was always a little upset with me. She was annoyed that I gave professional advice for managing Jessica when I had no children of my own. Also, she felt that I hadn't fully appreciated how difficult it was being Jessica's mother.

Several months after we concluded parent counseling, Mrs. Stiles learned that my wife was expecting our first child. What was Mrs. Stiles's reaction upon hearing the good news? She exclaimed, "I hope that Dr. Clark's kid is as mean as a snake! Then he'll know what I had to put up with!"

Although you may not have a "Jessica," chances are that you do have a child who isn't always an angel. *The Time-Out Solution* can help you become a more self-confident and effective parent. You'll learn many new methods for improving your child's behavior. As a result, your child will be better behaved and happier. Your life will be simpler and more pleasant.

This book is your guide for handling a variety of common behavior problems. We'll look at specific solutions to problems such as the following:

- Your three-year-old hits you when she doesn't get her way. You have tried scolding and spanking her, but her behavior is getting worse.
- It embarrasses and angers you when your ten-year-old daughter talks back to you whenever you ask her to do a simple chore. When you explain to her how impolite her "back talk" is, she mocks you.
- You dread Saturday mornings. Your twelve-year-old and eight-year-old regularly engage in Saturday morning arguing and fighting while watching television. You repeatedly warn them to stop arguing and fighting. But really you have nothing effective to back up your warnings.
- Your five-year-old daughter has started having tantrums. She is even having tantrums in the homes of your friends. You are tired of her behavior and tired of making excuses for her. You feel helpless to change her.

The behavioral approach to child rearing and discipline is very useful in understanding children and helping them to change. What is the behavioral approach? What is behavioral discipline? The *behavioral approach* states that your child's good and bad behavior are both learned. It also maintains that behavior can be "unlearned" or changed. *Behavioral discipline* offers specific tested methods, skills, procedures, and strategies for you to use in getting improved behavior from your child.

You can be optimistic about helping your child to change. Behavioral methods are extremely effective in changing all kinds of problem behavior. Child research studies show a 50 to 90 percent reduction in a wide variety of problem behaviors with the use of behavioral methods. As a parent and psychologist, I have considerable confidence in these methods. In fact, I have used nearly all the behavioral methods described in this book with my own children. These skills are easy for you to learn, and they work.

## HOW TO USE THIS BOOK

Read Chapters 1 through 8 before using these new strategies with your child. Understanding the methods, step-by-step instructions, and examples in these chapters will enable you to be successful in guiding your child to improved behavior. Also, you will learn to avoid common pitfalls and mistakes when managing your child.

At the end of each chapter is a section called "Main Points to Remember." These are the most important ideas and instructions contained in each chapter.

*The Time-Out Solution* is based on my professional practice as a psychologist, my personal experience as a parent, and the results of numerous parent-child research studies. Managing one's children is a challenging and sometimes humbling task, even for psychologists and family counselors. My wife (an elementary school teacher) and I began to use the methods of discipline and child management described in this book with our two sons when they were toddlers.

More than fifteen years after working with Mrs. Stiles and Jessica, I still think about Mrs. Stiles and her "good wishes" for my firstborn. I have continued to study child management, not only to help parents, but also because I certainly didn't want to be cursed with "a kid as mean as a snake"!

# THE
# TIME-OUT
# SOLUTION

# PART I
# GOOD PARENTING BREEDS GOOD CHILDREN

*This section outlines the basic rules for successfully improving your child's behavior. You'll also learn how to avoid four specific child-rearing mistakes that parents commonly make.*

*You'll sharpen your communication skills as a parent and learn to strengthen your child's good behavior by rewarding that behavior. This section also clearly describes methods of effective but mild punishment for stopping bad behavior.*

*As you read, actually practice these new methods and skills with your child in order to be a more effective and happy parent. Now, let's get started with the fundamentals of good parenting!*

# 1
# Why Kids Behave and Misbehave

Why do some children sail through childhood with few noticeable behavior problems, while others are a constant problem to their parents? Other children, as well as adults, find these "problem kids" obnoxious and either complain about them or avoid them. It's as though some problem kids lie awake at night plotting their next day's misbehavior.

As a psychologist, I've had a firsthand look at the feelings of frustration and failure that many parents experience. Frustrated parents also lie awake at night, desperate for some solutions.

Solutions do exist. With increased knowledge of the rules and methods for improving behavior, you can help your child be a better behaved and more agreeable family member.

Good and bad behavior are both shaped by the rewards your child receives. Sometimes parents "accidentally" reward and strengthen their child's bad behavior. Three-year-old Patrick may get to stay up well past his bedtime (a reward) if he "wears his parents down" with

3

relentless complaining and crying. Your child's bad behavior will grow stronger if you or other people reward it. Behavior that is not rewarded or is punished will grow weaker and be less likely to occur in the future.

You should follow three basic child-rearing rules. The rules look simple; you can easily see what your friends are doing wrong with *their* children. However, when you try to use these rules with *your* child, you can appreciate how difficult it is to be consistent and effective. Remember these rules!

---

### THREE CHILD-REARING RULES

**Rule 1.**   Reward good behavior (and do it quickly and often).

**Rule 2.**   Don't "accidentally" reward bad behavior.

**Rule 3.**   Punish some bad behavior (but use mild punishment only).

---

# THREE CHILD-REARING RULES
## Rule 1: Reward Good Behavior (and Do It Quickly and Often)

Children learn to talk, dress themselves, share toys, and do chores because they receive attention and other types of rewards from their parents and other people for doing so. As parents, we should frequently and abundantly reward the good behavior of our children.

An adult holds a job and in return receives a paycheck and recognition from others. A paycheck and recognition are powerful rewards for working. Most of us would stop working if we weren't rewarded for our effort. Rewards shape and determine our behavior and the behavior of our children. Rewards are also called reinforcers because they reinforce behavior.

When your child gets a reward for engaging in a particular behavior, that behavior is strengthened or reinforced. This means that the behavior is more likely to occur in the future. People repeat behavior for which they are rewarded. We continue going to work because we get paid. If your child behaves in a way that pleases you, be sure to strengthen that behavior by frequently rewarding it. What type of rewards should you use? Read on.

*Social rewards* are very effective in strengthening the desirable behavior of both children and adults. Social rewards include smiles, hugs, pats, kisses, words of praise, eye contact, and attention. A hug or a kind word is easy to give. That's good, because our children need lots of social rewards to strengthen their appropriate behavior.

Some parents are stingy with praise and attention. They may say that they are too busy or that their child ought to demonstrate good behavior without being rewarded for it. Parents who are stingy with smiles, hugs, and words of praise don't realize the powerful effect of frequently rewarding their child's desirable behavior. If four-year-old Emily straightens her room or helps you with chores, you need to tell her that you appreciate it. If you don't, she will be less likely to help with chores in the future.

Praise is more effective in strengthening your child's desirable behavior if you praise the specific behavior rather than your child. After your son cleans and straightens his room, praise his behavior by saying, "Your room looks great and you did such a good job cleaning it!" That statement of praise is more effective than saying, "You are a good boy." Develop the habit of praising the specific behavior or action that you want strengthened.

Besides social rewards, you can also give *material rewards* and *activity rewards,* such as a special dessert, a small toy, nickels and dimes, a trip to the Dairy

Queen, or getting to help their parents bake a cake. For most children, however, social rewards are much more powerful than material rewards. In addition, social rewards are more convenient for parents to use. You are the main source of rewards for your child.

| REWARDS CHILDREN LIKE | | |
|---|---|---|
| **Social Rewards** | **Activity Rewards, Including Privileges** | **Material Rewards** |
| Smiles | Play cards with parent | Ice-cream |
| Hugs | Go to park | Ball |
| Pats | Look at book with parent | Money |
| Attention | | Book |
| Touching | Help bake cookies | Jump rope |
| Clapping hands | Watch a late TV movie | Balloons |
| | Have a friend over | Yo-yo |
| Winks | Play ball with parent | Flashlight |
| Praise | Play a game together | Special dessert |
| "Good job" | Go out for pizza together | |
| "Well done" | | Record |

To be effective, rewards must immediately follow your child's desirable behavior. If your child takes out the trash (even if that is her regular chore), you should thank her immediately after the task is done—not an hour or so later. All of us like to receive rewards for good behavior as immediately as possible. Children often ask to receive material rewards before rather than after they do a chore or engage in a desirable behavior. If you sometimes use material rewards, be sure you give them only after the desirable behavior occurs. When you give a material reward or activity reward to your child, also give a social reward.

# Rule 2: Don't "Accidentally" Reward Bad Behavior

When you accidentally reward your child's misbehavior, that misbehavior is strengthened and is more likely to occur again in the future. Often, busy or preoccupied parents unintentionally reward their child for engaging in undesirable or inappropriate behavior. When parents reward bad behavior, they are causing future problems for themselves as well as for their children. This is probably one of the most common child-rearing mistakes parents make.

Your child may have learned that he can delay going to bed at night by complaining, crying, and becoming emotionally upset when you say it's bedtime. After his complaining and crying have become intolerable, have you ever given in and let him stay up longer? If you have given in, you have unintentionally rewarded him for crying and becoming emotionally upset. Complaining, crying, and getting upset then are more likely to occur in the future. This kind of behavior is learned and reinforced just as appropriate and desirable behavior are learned and reinforced. Don't reward bad behavior or behavior you don't want.

## TEACHING NATHAN TO WHINE

When five-year-old Nathan wants his mother's attention, especially when she is busy, he begins to whine. Mother finds his whining so unbearable that she stops whatever she is doing, scolds him for whining, and then asks what is troubling him. Nathan has learned that when he really wants his mother's attention, he first must whine and accept a mild scolding. Then he gets his mother's attention—a powerful reward for five-year-old Nathan. Mother has taught Nathan to whine.

Also, children teach parents to behave in certain ways. Nathan has taught his mother to give him attention when he whines. When she gives him attention, he rewards her by stopping his whining. Children and parents teach each other both appropriate and inappropriate behaviors.

## The Strong-Willed Child

The strong-willed child presents another example of how parents and others can accidentally reward bad behavior and cause that behavior to become a severe problem. Watching a child cry and have a temper tantrum is distressing and emotionally upsetting. To stop his persistent crying and tantrums, parents and other people eventually give in to his demands. Thus, the strong-willed child learns to force others to give in to his demands by causing them emotional pain and discomfort.

A strong-willed child may achieve considerable power and control over his parents and others. To get his way, he may engage in endless pestering and complaining, yelling and crying, or physical attacks on parents, siblings, and peers. Only when others give him what he wants will he stop causing them stress and emotional pain. With boundless energy and endurance, he forces his parents and others to reward his bad behavior. You can help the strong-willed child by using the methods and skills outlined in this book.

# Rule 3: Punish Some Bad Behavior (But Use Mild Punishment Only)

You sometimes need to use *mild punishment* to decrease or eliminate some unacceptable or dangerous behavior.

### CHRISTY LOSES HER TRICYCLE

Mother saw four-year-old Christy ride her new tricycle into the street. That was against the rule and the rule already had been explained to Christy.

Immediately, Mother walked out to the street, removed Christy from her tricycle, and harshly scolded her. Mother also said, "Christy, for riding in the street—you can't ride your tricycle for a week." The tricycle was put away. It was seven days before Christy could play with it again.

You dislike punishing your child. You would prefer to reward good behavior. However, correctly using mild punishment is often essential in helping your child. You'll learn about the use of mild punishment such as scolding, natural consequences, logical consequences, time-out, and behavior penalties. However, don't use severe punishment, such as grim threats, sarcasm, or hard spankings. This often complicates behavior problems.

## FOUR COMMON CHILD-REARING ERRORS

Do follow the basic child-rearing rules discussed previously. Also, avoid making the following four errors. These parenting errors can contribute to behavior problems or emotional problems in children.

---

**FOUR CHILD-REARING ERRORS TO AVOID**

**Error 1.**  Parents fail to reward good behavior.

**Error 2.**  Parents "accidentally" punish good behavior.

**Error 3.**  Parents "accidentally" reward bad behavior.

**Error 4.**  Parents fail to punish bad behavior (when mild punishment is indicated).

---

# Error 1: Parents Fail to Reward Good Behavior

Sarah, a fourth grader, walks up to her father carrying her report card. Father, in his easy chair, is busy reading the newspaper. Father fails to reward his daughter for getting good grades in school.

> SARAH:   I made pretty good grades this term. Would you like to see my report card, Dad?
>
> FATHER:  Yes, but let me finish reading the paper first. . . . Would you go and ask Mother if she paid the bills today?

# Error 2: Parents Accidentally Punish Good Behavior

Eight-year-old Brian wants to surprise Mother by washing the lunch dishes. Mother unintentionally says something punishing.

> BRIAN:   I washed the dishes, Mother. Are you glad?
>
> MOTHER:  It's about time you did something to help around here. Now, what about the pans on the stove? Did you forget them? . . .

# Error 3: Parents Accidentally Reward Bad Behavior

Six-year-old Stephanie and her parents are camping and have just arrived back at camp with groceries for lunch. Mother is hot, tired, and hungry.

> STEPHANIE:  I want to go swimming before lunch.
>
> MOTHER:     First we eat lunch and have a nap, then you can go swimming.
>
> STEPHANIE:  I'll cry if I can't go swimming!
>
> MOTHER:     Oh, Stephanie, anything but that! Go ahead and swim first.

## Error 4: Parents Fail to Punish Bad Behavior (When Mild Punishment Is Indicated)

Mother and Father are sitting in the family room. Both observe eleven-year-old Mark impulsively hit his younger brother on the ear. Neither parent scolds Mark or uses any other form of mild punishment for his aggressive behavior.

MOTHER:    I wish you would handle your son.
FATHER:    Boys will be boys!

## PHYSICAL PROBLEMS MAY CONTRIBUTE TO BEHAVIOR PROBLEMS

Being hungry or overly tired can temporarily lower your child's capacity for self-control and intensify his bad behavior. Certain medical conditions can also increase the likelihood of behavior problems. If you suspect that your child has a medical condition, take him to your family physician or pediatrician for a checkup.

Even though a chronic physical condition may contribute to your child's bad behavior, keep working on improving that behavior. All the rules and methods discussed in this book are suitable for helping children with handicaps or other physical problems. Succeeding chapters will show you when and how to use effective methods for helping your child to improve his behavior.

## REASONS PARENTS DON'T DISCIPLINE THEIR KIDS

There are various reasons why some parents avoid disciplining their children. These parents need to be aware of why they are hesitant to discipline and to overcome their resistance to disciplining. You can't expect your child to change a bad behavior if you are not first willing to change your own behavior. The following are some reasons why parents find it difficult to change their own behavior.

**The Hopeless Parent.** This parent feels that his child is unable to change and will always behave badly. He or she has given up on their child.

### IN AND OUT OF THE GARBAGE CAN

It was the end of the school day and Mrs. Williams had stopped to talk about her son, Kevin, with his first-grade teacher. Whenever possible, Mrs. Williams complained about her son's bad behavior to whomever would listen. However, she never attempted to actually discipline her young son.

While Mrs. Williams and Kevin's teacher were talking, Kevin was down the hall playing near a large open garbage can. Mrs. Williams said, "I can't do a thing with Kevin. He never does what he is supposed to do."

As mother and teacher talked, and as they continued to watch Kevin from a distance, Kevin crawled in and out of the large garbage can.

Kevin's teacher said, "Do you see what Kevin is doing? He is going in and out of that garbage can!" Mrs. Williams responded with "Yes, he is always doing something like that. Only yesterday, he jumped in a mud puddle and . . ."

Never once did Mrs. Williams give Kevin a command such as "Get out of the garbage can!" She never asked him to stop what he was doing. She never actively helped Kevin to improve his bad behavior. Mrs. Williams had given up on her young son.

**The Nonconfronting Parent.** This parent avoids confronting his child. He really doesn't expect his child to mind and his child realizes this. Sometimes this parent fears he will lose his child's love if he makes any demands on him. Hearing "I hate you," "You're a terrible father," or "I wish I had a new Daddy" completely devastates this parent and neutralizes his will to discipline.

**The Low-Energy Parent.** He or she can't seem to muster the parenting energy necessary to keep up with an active or misbehaving child. Sometimes, a mother or father is a single parent and holds a full-time job. Occasionally, the low-energy parent is suffering from a short-term or chronic depression.

**The Guilty Parent.** This parent blames himself or herself for the child's problems and feels especially guilty about attempts to discipline the child. Self-blame and guilt prevent this parent from teaching his or her child improved behavior. This parent becomes permissive and passive.

**The Angry Parent.** Many parents become emotionally upset and angry each time they discipline their child. Since they can't discipline without being angry and upset and feeling miserable as a consequence, they simply ignore their child's misbehavior. The time-out method, however, helps you to be composed when you correct your child.

**The Hindered Parent.** Sometimes a parent is hindered by a spouse when attempting to discipline their child. If this happens to you, continue talking with your spouse about desirable goals for your child. After agreeing on acceptable goals, work on agreeing on appropriate methods of discipline. Sometimes relatives or friends interfere with discipline. Frequently the same people who get upset if you do discipline your child, also get upset if you don't discipline your child. Don't let others discourage you from being an effective and self-confident parent.

**The Troubled Parent.** Marital problems and other difficult life situations sometimes become a heavy burden for a parent. Often, this parent lacks sufficient energy, time, and motivation to help his or her child.

Parenting a child and holding a family together is one of the most difficult and challenging tasks you will ever face. Psychologists and other professionals can help parents gain increased understanding of themselves and their family and can help them improve their parenting skills.

## MAIN POINTS TO REMEMBER

- Both good and bad behavior are strengthened when rewarded.
- Reward your child's good behavior quickly and often.
- Avoid rewarding your child's bad behavior.
- Use mild punishment to decrease or eliminate some bad behavior.
- Your child needs your discipline as well as your love. If something is preventing you from disciplining your child, determine what it is and work toward correcting it.

# 2
# Clear Communication Promotes Effective Parenting

Clear and frequent communication between spouses promotes effective parenting. Likewise, clear communication between you and your child is also essential for helping improve her behavior. Good communication requires a lot of talking and listening by all family members. Your child needs clear communication, discipline, and lots of love from you.

## PARENTS MUST AGREE ON GOALS

You and your spouse must determine which elements of your child's behavior are good or desirable and which are bad or undesirable. Your basic values determine the goals and standards of behavior you set for your child. Reward and strengthen your child's good behavior and eliminate or weaken her unacceptable behavior by failing to reward it.

## BOTH REWARDING AND PUNISHING
## DAVID'S BABY TALK

When four-year-old David wanted something or just wanted attention, he often used "baby talk." If he was thirsty, he would point to the kitchen faucet and say, "wa-wa." David's mother thought his baby talk was cute and often rewarded it (getting him a drink of water when he said "wa-wa"). David's father thought his baby talk was obnoxious, scolded him for it, and called him a "sissy."

David was being rewarded *and* punished for using baby talk. As the days passed, David became more and more emotional, cried easily, and began avoiding his father.

Rewarding and punishing a child for the same behavior is unfair and may cause emotional or behavior problems. Both parents need to decide which behavior is desirable and which is undesirable.

If you are a single parent, clarify your goals and set realistic expectations for your child's behavior by frequently talking with another adult who also cares for your child. Grandparents or a baby-sitter may be helping to rear your child on a day-to-day basis. If so, be sure that you and the other adult have consistent expectations and goals for your child.

# CLEAR COMMUNICATION
# BETWEEN PARENT AND CHILD

Both you and your spouse need to jointly determine the rules you want your child to follow. When possible, encourage your child to participate in making or modifying rules. If your child helps set a rule, she is more likely to follow it and less likely to resent it. Once a rule is decided, however, you should expect her to follow it. Your child needs to know which of her behaviors you like and which ones are unacceptable. Of course, never tell your child that she is a "bad child." However, do tell her which behavior you consider bad or intolerable.

### THE TWINS HELP SET A RULE

Gregory and Adam, four-year-old twins, loved to roughhouse and wrestle with each other in the house. Wrestling in the house was okay when they were two years old and when they were very small. However, they were growing rapidly and the house was taking a beating.

Mother and Father sat down with them and explained that they were "bigger now" and that a new rule was needed. The twins asked, "Can we wrestle in the family room if we don't do it anyplace else?" Their parents agreed and a new rule was born: "No wrestling anywhere in the house—except in the family room."

Whenever you establish a rule, your children should know the rule well enough to repeat it when asked to do so. The parents of Gregory and Adam helped their twins learn the rule by saying it with them. Mother or Father could ask, "What is the rule about wrestling?" and either Gregory or Adam would respond, "The rule is—no wrestling anywhere in the house, except in the family room."

# HOW TO GIVE
# EFFECTIVE COMMANDS

"Please pick up your toys" is a *simple request*. "Stop throwing food!" and "Come here and hang up the coat that you threw on the floor!" are *commands*.

Parents of children who don't mind are often unable to give clear, emphatic directives or commands to their children. All parents, especially parents of hard-to-handle children, must be able to give clear, effective instructions or commands. If you use time-out, an especially effective method of discipline, you must be able to tell your child, "Go to time-out immediately!" Learning to give commands doesn't mean that you should start barking orders like a drill sergeant or that your ten-year-old is about to enter basic training. However, if your child usually doesn't mind and even sasses you when you scold her for not minding, you must be able to give clear, effective commands and to back up your commands.

When are commands given? Give your child a command when you want her to stop a specific misbehavior and you believe that she might disobey a simple request to stop the misbehavior. Also, give a command when you want your child to start a particular behavior and you believe that your child might disobey a simple request to start the behavior.

How should you give a command? Assume that you come into the living room and find Jennifer, your "hard-to-handle" seven-year-old, jumping up and down on your new sofa. You should walk right up to her, have a stern facial expression, look her in the eye, and maintain eye contact. Call her name and then give her a clear, direct command in a firm tone of voice: "Jennifer, jumping on the furniture is against the rule. Get off the sofa!" You have given her a clear command.

Give clear, explicit commands rather than vague ones. Your child is more likely to mind if you say, "Come here and start putting those toys on the shelf!" She is less likely to comply with a vague statement such as, "Do something with all those toys!"

Don't ask a question or make an indirect comment when you give a command such as, "It's not nice to jump on the sofa." Don't say to Jennifer, "Why are you jumping on the sofa?" She just might smile at you and say, "Because it's lots of fun!"

Also, don't give your reasons for a rule while the bad behavior is taking place. The time to explain a rule is before your child breaks it or after the bad behavior stops. Do not say to Jennifer while she is still bouncing up and down, "You shouldn't be jumping on the sofa. It cost a lot of money. We still owe the finance company on it. The springs might come loose. . . ." However, do say to Jennifer, "Get off the sofa!"

After you give your command, Jennifer will probably decide to mind you and get off the sofa. However, let's assume that Jennifer decides to disobey your command. She may decide to test you and see if you have anything with which to back up your command. It's not necessary to severely punish or threaten to punish Jennifer in order to back up your command. This might further complicate an already difficult parent-child problem.

You have a very simple and effective backup for your command. You have "time-out!" Later, in Part II, we'll discuss how to use time-out in such a confrontation—without getting intensely angry. For now, remember the following simple steps for giving effective commands. Memorize and, if necessary, practice these steps.

---

### GIVING EFFECTIVE COMMANDS TO YOUR CHILD

**Steps to follow:**

- Move close to your child.
- Have a stern facial expression.
- Say his or her name.
- Get and maintain eye contact.
- Use a firm tone of voice.
- Give a direct, simple, and clear command.
- "Back up" your command, if necessary.

# CHILDREN NEED DISCIPLINE AND LOTS OF LOVE

Discipline means teaching a child self-control and improved behavior. Your child learns self-respect and self-
control by receiving both love and discipline from you.
We discipline our children because we love them and
we want them to become responsible, competent adults.
Being an effective parent requires love, knowledge,
effort, and time. This book will teach you basic principles for changing behavior and practical skills for helping your child. To actually help your child, however, you
must practice these skills and you must provide effort
and time, as well as love.

# MAIN POINTS TO REMEMBER

- Parents must agree about which of their child's behaviors are desirable and which are undesirable.
- You and your child must communicate clearly with
  each other.
- You must be able to give clear, effective instructions
  and commands.

# 3
# Ways to Increase Your Child's Good Behavior

Do you remember teaching a child how to tie his shoes? You first showed him how to do it. Then you asked him to try. When he attempted this new task, you gave him lots of attention and encouragement. He responded by working even harder to please you.

Your encouragement, close attention, smiles, hugs, pats, and words of approval are extremely important to your child and strengthen his behavior. This chapter will show you how to reward your child to get good behavior from him.

Just as it's important to reward your child's good behavior, it's also important to *fail to reward bad behavior*. When you see behavior that you don't want your child to continue, be sure that you actively ignore it.

## ACTIVELY IGNORE YOUR CHILD'S BAD BEHAVIOR

*Active ignoring* is briefly removing all attention from your misbehaving child. Active ignoring is being sure that you don't accidentally reward his bad behavior

21

with attention. This method of managing children is particularly effective in reducing the tantrums of toddlers and preschoolers. If you scold or attend to your child while he is having a tantrum, you might unintentionally reward that behavior. Try active ignoring to weaken his behavior. If your child is in a safe place, walk out of the room and wait until his tantrum ceases before returning. Or, you might turn your back and pretend to be absorbed in something else. When his bad behavior stops, give him lots of attention. Also, be sure that your child's bad behavior doesn't drive you into giving him a material reward (such as cookies before dinner) or an activity reward (such as watching a late TV movie on a school night).

Use active ignoring to weaken these ways of misbehaving:

- Whining and fussing
- Pouting and sulking
- Loud crying intended to punish parents
- Loud complaining
- Insistent begging and demanding
- Breath-holding and mild tantrums

How do you actively ignore your child? Follow the points listed in the table on the opposite page.

Active ignoring often helps to reduce misbehavior. However, when it doesn't, consider using one of the other methods described in this chapter or in succeeding chapters.

## REWARD GOOD ALTERNATIVE BEHAVIOR

If your child's undesirable "target behavior" is whining, then the alternative behavior is talking in a normal tone of voice. If your child normally whines when he wants

---

### ACTIVELY IGNORE SOME MISBEHAVIORS

**Guidelines to follow:**

- Briefly remove all attention from your child.

- Refuse to argue, scold, or talk.

- Turn your head and avoid eye contact.

- Don't show anger in your manner or gestures.

- Act absorbed in some other activity—or leave the room.

- Be sure your child's bad behavior doesn't get him or her a material reward.

- Give your child lots of attention when the bad behavior stops.

---

something, then you should praise him when he asks for something without whining. *Reward your child's alternative behavior in order to strengthen it.*

Assume that Christopher, your four-year-old, usually has a temper tantrum when he doesn't get what he wants—for example, when he doesn't get a cookie just before dinner. The next time you turn down one of his requests, be sure to reward him with praise if he demonstrates self-control. Say to him, "Christopher, you didn't get a cookie this time, but you acted grown-up anyway. I'm proud of that grown-up behavior. After we eat dinner you may have three cookies!"

What behavior has to go? What is the behavior you want? Wait for that good behavior. Then "catch your child being good" and reward him. If your child doesn't seem to know how to do the desirable behavior, such as sharing or trading toys, teach it to him. Teaching the desirable behavior is discussed next.

## REWARDING GOOD ALTERNATIVE BEHAVIOR—EXAMPLES FOR PARENTS

| Target Behavior to Be Decreased (Use Active Ignoring or Mild Punishment) | Good Behavior to Be Increased (Use Praise and Attention) |
|---|---|
| • Whining | • Talking in a normal tone of voice |
| • Grabbing toys | • Sharing toys; trading toys |
| • Temper tantrums when frustrated | • Self-control when frustrated |
| • Hostile teasing | • Playing cooperatively |
| • Swearing | • Talking without swearing |
| • Hitting | • Solving problems using words |

# HELP YOUR CHILD PRACTICE GOOD BEHAVIOR

Help your child practice the behavior that you want him to learn. For example, if your child grabs toys away from another child, tell him to trade toys instead. Then demonstrate toy trading yourself and help him to actually practice this skill.

### TOY-GRABBING GLORIA

When three-year-old Gloria wanted a toy from her baby sister, she often grabbed it. Gloria's parents didn't allow her to keep the toy because that rewarded her for grabbing toys. However, Gloria persisted.

To help his daughter change, Mr. Scott developed a two-part plan. For the first part, Gloria either received a scolding or a time-out when she grabbed a toy.

For the second part, Mr. Scott helped Gloria learn to trade toys. If Gloria wanted a toy truck from her sister, she showed her another toy and then offered to trade toys. Sometimes Gloria offered four or five different toys before her baby sister finally wanted to trade.

Mr. Scott taught Gloria the skill of toy trading by first demonstrating this skill himself and by having her watch. He traded toys with the baby. Then Gloria practiced with the baby and Mr. Scott watched. When Gloria was successful, he praised her efforts. However, when Gloria grabbed a toy from her baby sister, he scolded her or placed her in time-out.

Gloria became good at toy trading and also spent more time sharing toys and playing with her sister. Mr. Scott weakened toy grabbing by using a mild punishment. He taught Gloria toy trading to replace toy grabbing.

## USE GRANDMA'S RULE

Help your children perform unpleasant tasks by using Grandma's Rule. *Grandma's Rule* states, "After you do your chore, then you get to play." It's easier to begin and complete an unpleasant task if we get to have fun afterward.

Don't reverse Grandma's Rule. An example of reversing Grandma's Rule is to say, "You can watch television now if you promise to do your math homework later tonight." If your child always procrastinates with his math because he hates it, he won't be motivated to finish it by first watching television. He will continue avoiding his math. He will also feel guilty or upset for failing to complete it. Promises to begin a task and guilt don't help children do unpleasant chores. Having fun afterward is a good motivator.

Getting your child to do something extremely distasteful when reversing Grandma's Rule is difficult to do—like driving your car somewhere backward. Use Grandma's Rule correctly.

| USING GRANDMA'S RULE—EXAMPLES FOR PARENTS | |
|---|---|
| **After You . . .** | **Then You Get To . . .** |
| • complete your math homework | • watch television. |
| • wash the supper dishes | • go out and play ball. |
| • straighten your room | • play video games. |
| • take a nap | • go swimming. |
| • eat your vegetables | • eat dessert. |
| • practice the piano for twenty minutes | • visit a friend. |

## SET A GOOD EXAMPLE

Parents constantly demonstrate or "model" behavior that their children observe. Your child learns how to behave and misbehave by observing and imitating your behavior and the behavior of others. Don't unintentionally demonstrate behavior that you wouldn't like to see in your child.

Your child pays particularly close attention to you when you are frustrated with a problem or having a conflict with another person. By watching you, he is learning how he might handle his own frustrations and conflicts with others in the future.

If you use a lot of sarcasm and criticism in dealing with other people, you're actually teaching your child to use sassy talk and complaining as a way of dealing with you and other people. By watching their parents, some kids learn that people swear if they get hurt. Sometimes children even learn to have temper tantrums by watching their parents lose control of their own emotions and behavior. You are a role model for your child whether you want to be or not. Be a good role model!

Children also learn by watching people on television and in the movies. Many programs show people trying to solve problems and conflicts with others by using aggression and violence. Monitor the kind of television programs and movies your kids watch.

## BE AN ORGANIZED PARENT

Be organized and plan ahead to be an effective parent. Anticipate your child's needs before his bad behavior forces you to meet his needs. When you allow your child's bad behavior to force you to meet his needs, you might unintentionally reward that bad behavior.

If you are shopping with your children, return home before they are completely exhausted. The time to have a long telephone conversation is not just before supper when your children are hungry and fussing with each other. If you and your child are spending the evening visiting friends, avoid staying hours past your child's normal bedtime.

Your children, especially if they are young, need a lot of care and supervision. As parents, we really don't go off duty until our children are asleep, and even then we are on call. A favorite time of the day for busy mothers and fathers is after the children are asleep.

## MAIN POINTS TO REMEMBER

- Encourage and praise your child's good behavior.
- Actively ignore some misbehaviors.
- After targeting an undesirable behavior, reward the good alternative behavior.
- Help your child to practice behavior you want him to learn.
- Use Grandma's Rule to help your child perform unpleasant chores.
- Set a good example for your child.

# 4
# Major Methods for Stopping Bad Behavior

## QUESTIONS PARENTS ASK
## ABOUT PUNISHMENT

- "Should I use mild punishment to change my child's misbehavior?"
- "What kinds of mild punishment are effective in stopping misbehavior?"
- "Can the use of punishment be emotionally harmful to my child?"
- "Why do my children continue to misbehave after they are punished?"

You can use five types of mild punishment to help your child. One of these methods, time-out, is brief and especially effective in stopping persistent misbehavior that is impulsive, explosive, and hard to handle.

Other chapters in this book describe, step by step, when and how to use the time-out method. Time-out does have a limitation: when you use time-out, you should use it immediately after the bad behavior occurs. But what should you do about serious misbehavior which you discover minutes or hours later?

Four other methods of mild punishment are effective even if you can't apply them immediately: (1) scolding and disapproval, (2) natural consequences, (3) logical consequences, and (4) behavior penalty. This chapter will describe how you can correctly use these methods.

To be a confident and competent parent, you must know and use several methods to manage your child's problem behavior. You can easily learn these effective methods. It's a lot easier to deal with a particular misbehavior if you know several ways to handle it.

Mild punishment can stop or weaken your child's bad behavior. However, it can't increase good behavior when used alone. As emphasized in earlier chapters, you also must *frequently reward your child's good behavior.*

---

## GUIDELINES FOR PARENTS WHEN USING MILD PUNISHMENT

**Points to remember:**

- Use punishment sparingly.

- Use mild punishment only.

- Punish quickly after the bad behavior occurs.

- Punish when you are in control of yourself.

- Briefly state a reason for the punishment.

- Avoid physical punishment.

---

*Punishment* is an unpleasant consequence or penalty that follows a behavior. When you use punishment, be sure to observe the correct guidelines.

The correct use of mild punishment won't emotionally harm your child. Often it is essential for improving her behavior. However, severe punishment, sarcasm, and threats can damage your child's self-concept and

emotional well-being. Children who are severely punished may become extremely withdrawn or may act
more aggressive and belligerent toward others. Mothers
and fathers who severely discipline their children frequently carry a heavy burden of guilt.

## BEING A RATIONAL AND
## NONAGGRESSIVE MODEL

When at their wits' end, parents often try to punish or
control their kids by making irrational threats such as,
"You're grounded all summer for doing that!" or "I'm
going to pull every hair from your head unless you . . . !"
Parents who use severe or frequent spankings often
don't realize that several different methods of mild
punishment can be more effective in changing behavior.

Your child will imitate your behavior. If you shout,
make irrational threats, or spank, you are "modeling"
this behavior for your child to imitate. She may yell,
become emotional, or attempt to "manage" others physically. When using time-out discipline, you are a rational and nonaggressive role model for your child.

Your job as a parent is often stressful and upsetting.
Sometimes your child may intentionally try to anger
you. Children enjoy getting attention and controlling
their parents by making them angry and emotional.
However, you can resist yielding to your anger. You *can*
do it. You can avoid yelling and screaming, making
grim threats, using sarcasm, giving harsh spankings, or
using other forms of severe or ineffective punishment.
Examine the following methods of discipline.

## USING TIME-OUT TO STOP
## BAD BEHAVIOR

In basketball and football, *time-out* is a brief interruption or suspension of play for participants. As a method

of discipline, time-out is a brief interruption of activities for your child.

*Time-out* means time-out from reinforcement, rewards, and attention. You quickly remove your child from the reinforcing or pleasurable situation in which the misbehavior occurs and briefly place her in a quiet and boring area that is not reinforcing or enjoyable at all. By placing your child in time-out, you prevent her from getting attention or other rewards following her undesirable behavior.

---

### ADVANTAGES OF USING THE TIME-OUT METHOD

- Time-out quickly weakens many types of bad behavior.

- Time-out helps stop some kinds of misbehavior permanently. Behavior then improves.

- It's easy for parents to learn and use.

- Parents report feeling less angry and upset when using this method of discipline.

- Parents are a rational and nonaggressive "model" for their children.

- The parent-child relationship quickly returns to normal following the use of time-out.

---

The time-out method of discipline has two goals, an immediate one and a long-term one. The immediate goal is to bring an abrupt stop to the problem behavior. The long-term goal of time-out is to help your child to achieve self-discipline.

Children don't like time-out because they experience a number of immediate losses even though these losses are brief. When placed in time-out, kids lose attention from their family. They lose power and control and the ability to anger and upset their parents. Kids lose the freedom to play with toys and games and to join interesting activities. Since the time-out method is swift and definite, kids are less able to avoid this form of discipline. Your child will usually be irritated with you when sent to time-out and during time-out. Ordinarily, your child's annoyance will rapidly disappear after time-out is over.

### "I'D RATHER GET A SPANKING!"

Mr. Gordon used the time-out method for several months and was successful in keeping his five-year-old son, Sammie, from hitting and pushing. Mr. Gordon greatly decreased his use of swats, spankings, and intense scoldings. He was interested in his son's feelings regarding time-out versus more aggressive forms of discipline.

On a quiet Saturday afternoon, Mr. Gordon casually asked, "Sammie, when you hit your little brother, what should Dad do? Spank you or put you in time-out?" Sammie replied, "I'd rather get a spanking! I want to get it over with. There is nothing to do in time-out. I don't like time-out!"

The time-out method is effective in correcting bad behavior because kids hate being in time-out. Many children prefer to get a spanking or a severe scolding rather than briefly being placed in time-out.

Both children and adults resist changing their behavior. Kids don't want to stop their troublesome behavior. However, if they continue with these kinds of problem behavior, they receive repeated time-outs. Consequently, they find these problem behaviors easier to give up. Kids then explore different ways to meet their needs. When these new behaviors are rewarded, they are strengthened and more likely to occur in the future.

Time-out weakens your child's old problem behaviors and encourages new acceptable behavior to emerge.

You can successfully use the time-out method if your child is between two and twelve years old. However, when you begin using time-out with your child, he shouldn't be older than eleven years old. Time-out, when correctly used, is safe and effective in stopping bad behavior. However, parents often make various mistakes. The next chapter describes the exact steps for correctly using time-out.

## USING SCOLDING AND DISAPPROVAL CORRECTLY

### THE MISSING COOKIES

Mother just discovered that seven-year-old Michelle had disobeyed her and eaten most of the chocolate chip cookies being saved for dessert. She walked toward her daughter and in a stern voice said, "Michelle, I'm very disappointed that you ate the cookies. I was saving them for supper. Now we won't have enough for dessert tonight."

Michelle's mother correctly used disapproval, a form of mild punishment commonly used by parents. When you are scolding for bad behavior, move close to your child, look her in the eye, be stern, express your feelings, and name the undesirable behavior. It's important to have self-control and to avoid making sarcastic or belittling remarks.

Be brief and calm when scolding your child. Some children enjoy a lengthy tongue-lashing and watching their parent become upset. They like getting the extra attention from their mother or father, even if that attention is negative.

Avoid nattering at your child when you want her to improve the bad behavior. *Nattering* is a combination of chattering, nagging, scolding, and complaining. For example, her mother might have said to Michelle, "I'm mad that you ate all the cookies that I was saving for dessert. Another thing, your hair is a mess again and you left all your toys in the living room. You never appreciate what I do for you. Furthermore . . ." Nattering doesn't help your child improve the problem behavior and it weakens your relationship. Don't natter at your child!

Remember to show disapproval of your child's behavior and not of your child. Don't criticize her personality or character. Let her know that you still respect and love her as a person. Instead of saying "You are a mean girl for hitting your brother," say "It was mean to hit your brother." Don't say "You are a naughty girl." Do say "That was a naughty thing to do." When you scold, be sure to disapprove of your child's behavior and not of your child.

An effective time to use disapproval is just as your child's misbehavior is getting started. For example, your two children may begin with playful teasing and then rapidly move on to hostile teasing. When you find this happening, quickly express disapproval. You might say, "I really don't like the teasing that's going on between the two of you. I don't mind a little teasing, but when it continues you two frequently get into an argument. I don't want to hear any more teasing this evening!"

For many children, disapproval is normally sufficient when used alone as a mild punishment. However, if your child usually becomes angry and argues when you scold him or smiles at you, then scolding isn't very effective. When scolding and disapproval are not effective, consider using time-out or another form of mild punishment.

Signs that scolding and disapproval are not effective with your child:

- Your child usually scolds back, sasses, mocks, or argues with you.
- Your child smiles, ignores you, or appears inattentive.

- She has a temper tantrum when scolded.
- She seems to enjoy getting the extra attention from you, even though it's negative attention.

## NATURAL CONSEQUENCES FOR BAD BEHAVIOR

A natural consequence for not wearing gloves on a cold day is having cold hands. Staying late after school is a natural consequence for not doing a homework assignment.

A *natural consequence* is an event that normally or naturally happens to your child following his bad behavior, unless you step in to prevent the consequence. You allow your child to experience the natural consequences of his own behavior unless there is some danger to his safety.

If six-year-old James teases a friend, his friend may get angry and go home. James will be left without a playmate. Being alone is a natural consequence of teasing one's friend. Consider the various examples of natural consequences for bad behavior described in the box, "Allowing Natural Consequences to Occur for Bad Behavior."

Parents who use natural consequences believe that children learn to improve their behavior when they are allowed to experience consequences that naturally follow their own decisions and actions. Since punishment is delivered by nature and not by parents, children are much less likely to get angry at their parents for being punished.

## LOGICAL CONSEQUENCES FOR BAD BEHAVIOR

Sometimes you can't allow natural consequences to occur because it's dangerous to your child. For example, Father can't allow three-year-old John to experi-

## ALLOWING NATURAL CONSEQUENCES TO OCCUR FOR BAD BEHAVIOR— EXAMPLES FOR PARENTS

| Bad Behavior | Natural Consequences |
| --- | --- |
| • Handling a cat roughly | • Getting scratched |
| • Breaking a toy on purpose | • Having a broken toy which is not replaced with a new one |
| • Teasing neighborhood children | • Being avoided by neighborhood children |
| • Not doing a homework assignment | • Staying after school the next day if required by the teacher |
| • Not wearing gloves on a cold day | • Having cold hands |
| • Not combing your hair | • Being told by other children that your hair is a mess |
| • Getting ready for school very slowly in the morning | • Being late for school and explaining to the teacher why you are late |
| • Pushing and shoving other children of the same age | • Getting pushed and shoved back |
| • Carelessly spilling a drink | • Not getting a refill |

ence natural consequences for riding a tricycle into the street. However, Father can apply a logical consequence—if John doesn't ride his tricycle in a safe place, then he loses the privilege of riding his tricycle for a time. Father can quickly remove the tricycle and not allow John to use it for one week.

When using *logical consequences* to handle problem behavior, you provide punishment for the bad behavior.

## APPLYING LOGICAL CONSEQUENCES FOR BAD BEHAVIOR—EXAMPLES FOR PARENTS

| Bad Behavior | Logical Consequences |
|---|---|
| • Riding a tricycle into the street | • Tricycle is put up for one week |
| • Chewing gum gets stuck to furniture, clothes, or hair | • No more gum for five days |
| • Swearing on the telephone | • Can't phone out for three days |
| • Mistreating or refusal to care for one's pet | • Placing the pet in another home, after several warnings and discussions |
| • Refusal to brush teeth regularly | • No more candy or soft drinks until regular tooth brushing is begun |
| • Brother and sister argue and fuss all morning | • Family outing to the park is cancelled that afternoon |
| • Not eating the main course at supper | • No dessert |

Also, you need to make sure that the punishment logically fits the nature of your child's misbehavior. The punishment is a logical or sensible consequence considering the particular bad behavior. When your child sees a clear and reasonable relationship between her bad behavior and the punishment, she is more likely to change her behavior. In addition, she is less likely to resent the punishment.

When you apply a logical consequence, it is important to avoid a consequence that is too severe or lasts too long. For example, the consequence of "No tricycle for two months!" is too harsh for a three-year-old who rides his tricycle into the street. When angry or emotionally upset by your child's misbehavior, you might declare a consequence that is too extreme. If you make this common mistake, there is a simple solution: merely tell your child that you made the consequence too severe and that you have reduced the consequence.

The box, "Applying Logical Consequences for Bad Behavior," gives examples of parents using this method of discipline.

## BEHAVIOR PENALTIES FOR BAD BEHAVIOR

If you can't think of a logical consequence for a particular misbehavior, then consider using *behavior penalty*. Behavior penalty is another method of punishment that is effective, but mild. Your child receives some penalty (such as no television for two days) following some specific bad behavior (such as lying to you).

The penalty consists of a loss of certain privileges, a fine, or an extra chore that your child finds especially distasteful. The penalty is not "logically" related to the bad behavior. For example, each time that nine-year-old Heather mistreats her puppy, she loses the privilege of playing her stereo for the rest of that day. The temporary loss of her stereo (the penalty) is not logically related to mistreating her puppy (the behavior). In selecting an effective penalty, Heather's parents need to know what kind of penalty is most meaningful for Heather. "No bicycle riding for two days!" is an ineffective penalty if Heather rarely rides her bike anyway.

When you use behavior penalty, try to state the penalty before the specific bad behavior occurs. For example, Heather's mother might say, "Heather, your father and I have talked about the way you sometimes mistreat your puppy. In the future when you mistreat Scottie, you'll lose the use of your stereo for the rest of the day." Mother should have Heather state out loud the misbehavior and the behavior penalty. This will help her to remember to be kind to Scottie.

The box, "Behavior Penalties for Bad Behavior," gives

## BEHAVIOR PENALTIES FOR BAD BEHAVIOR— EXAMPLES FOR PARENTS

| Behavior | Penalty |
| --- | --- |
| • Tattling on other children | • Having to immediately write three times, "Kids don't like it when I tattle." |
| • Swearing | • A 25-cent fine for each swear word |
| • Lying to parents | • No television for two days |
| • Fighting with neighborhood children | • No bicycle riding for a week |
| • Persistent teasing of little brother | • Stereo and records are "put up" for three days |
| • Failure to clean up one's bedroom by 5:00 P.M. | • No playing outdoors that evening |

examples of parents using this method of mild punishment.

In situations where it is not practical to use natural consequences or logical consequences to handle misbehavior, consider using behavior penalty. Avoid making the penalty too severe or too lengthy, however.

The box, "Methods of Mild Punishment," provides a brief comparison of the five methods of mild punishment discussed in this chapter. These five methods are the most effective forms of mild punishment you can use. To be successful in handling different types of misbehavior, you should know how to use all five methods.

Time-out is extremely effective, but it should be used only with children between the ages of two and twelve. Also, you should apply time-out immediately after the bad behavior occurs. Many parents admit that the most difficult behaviors to handle frequently occur right under their noses. Time-out is particularly helpful in stopping these persistent misbehaviors.

The other methods of mild punishment may be used with children who fall within a wide range of ages. These other methods are also most effective if applied as quickly as possible after the misbehavior occurs. However, these methods are still rather effective if applied minutes or a few hours after the misbehavior is discovered.

Avoid expressing intense anger when you use punishment. Your child should believe that she got punished because she behaved badly and not because you got angry.

## BAD BEHAVIOR
## SOMETIMES PERSISTS

Often, children will persist in bad behavior. There are various reasons for this. The amount of reward the child receives for the bad behavior may far outweigh the punishment. Nicole may tattle on her brother and

## METHODS OF MILD PUNISHMENT—COMPARISON FOR PARENTS

| Method of Mild Punishment | Age of Child | Effectiveness of Punishment | Type of Behavior Punished | How Quickly Applied |
|---|---|---|---|---|
| Time-Out | Two through twelve years | Extremely effective | Most behavior, especially hard-to-handle behavior | Immediately, if possible |
| Scolding and Disapproval | All ages | Moderately effective | All behavior | Immediately or later |
| Natural Consequences | All ages | Effective | Some behavior | Immediately or later |
| Logical Consequences | Three through adolescence | Effective | Most behavior | Immediately or later |
| Behavior Penalty | Five through adolescence | Effective | All behavior | Immediately or later |

enjoy getting him into trouble even though Mother shows disapproval for her tattling. In this case, Nicole's reward (getting her brother into trouble) outweighs her punishment (receiving disapproval).

Perhaps a child has learned that he runs very little risk of actually being punished. For instance, Aaron occasionally raids the cookie jar, but rarely gets caught. If he is caught, his parents may only threaten to punish, but never follow through with actual punishment.

Sometimes parents demonstrate a particular behavior themselves—such as swearing—for which they punish their child. Children tend to imitate their parents' behavior even if their parents punish them for that behavior.

As a parent, be consistent in the types of behavior that you reward and the behavior that you punish. When you do punish, use punishment that is both mild and effective.

## MAIN POINTS TO REMEMBER

- Rewarding good behavior is the easiest and best way to produce desirable behavior.
- Mild punishment helps stop your child's bad behavior.
- Use punishment sparingly and use mild punishment only.
- Be a rational and nonaggressive model when you use punishment.
- The most effective methods of mild punishment are time-out, scolding and disapproval, natural consequences, logical consequences, and behavior penalties.

# PART II
# BASIC SKILLS FOR THE TIME-OUT METHOD

*Time-out is a powerful method for stopping bad behavior. In this section, you'll learn the basic skills for correctly using time-out. Each chapter describes separate steps. If you have questions or problems regarding a particular step, you can review the chapter describing that step. The chapters have separate instructions for managing very young children who are two to four years old, and for older children who are five to twelve years old.*

*Since parents ask many questions about the correct use of time-out, I have included many examples. The chapters summarize and repeat important points. If you think your child might not cooperate with the time-out method, refer to Chapter 8 for solutions.*

*Let's get started with the time-out method!*

# 5
# Getting Started with Time-Out

## TIME-OUT QUESTIONS PARENTS ASK

- "Which of my child's bad behavior can be decreased by the time-out method?"
- "What are the steps for correctly using time-out?"
- "How long should my child spend in time-out?"
- "Could time-out be emotionally damaging to my child?"

You can do it! You can help your child to improve his behavior. Using the time-out method, you and your spouse can be more effective and self-confident parents.

You may use time-out with children between the ages of two and twelve years, as mentioned in the previous chapter. This chapter outlines the *time-out and ten-word and ten-second method* and tells you the basic steps to follow in correctly using time-out for the first time. Other chapters of this book will explain each of these steps.

Immediately place your child in time-out after the

undesirable target behavior—such as hitting or sassy talk. Send him there using no more than *ten words and ten seconds*. He stays one minute in time-out for each year of age.

Remember! Ten words or less, ten seconds or less in getting there, and one minute in time-out for each year of age. By using the time-out and ten-ten method, you can be consistent, fair, and effective in helping your child to learn acceptable behavior.

Set a timer for the same number of minutes each time that you place your child in time-out. Always use a small portable timer that can ring. If you don't have a portable timer now, put one on your shopping list today. You can get one at most hardware and department stores. The timer keeps accurate track of the time and signals your child when he may leave time-out. *Not using a portable timer is one of the most common mistakes parents make.*

The steps of the time-out method and the number of minutes in time-out are always the same, no matter what your child did. In addition to being effective in changing bad behavior, time-out is easy to use. In fact, unlike other methods of discipline, you will find that time-out gets easier and easier as you use it.

## TIME-OUT WON'T HARM YOUR CHILD

Some parents are afraid to use time-out because they wonder if this form of discipline might cause their child to develop emotional problems. Although children hate time-out, this means of discipline won't harm your child. The time-out method is often an essential tool in helping children to grow out of their emotional and behavioral problems. However, when you use time-out, be sure that you don't make any of the time-out mistakes described in Chapter 8.

# OBSERVE THE
# BAD BEHAVIOR YOURSELF

Ideally, you should see or hear the bad behavior so that you may immediately send your child to time-out. To be most effective, place your child in time-out within ten seconds after the bad behavior. Immediacy of time-out is especially important if your child is between two and four years old.

Bad behavior repeats itself. If you just missed an opportunity to time-out a bad behavior, be patient. Another misbehavior is likely to occur very soon!

# WHICH KINDS OF MISBEHAVIOR
# DESERVE TIME-OUT?

Time-out is effective in helping to correct your child's persistent misbehaviors that are impulsive, aggressive, emotional, or hostile. When time-out is compared with other methods of discipline, it is one of the most effective methods available for eliminating severe problem behaviors. However, recognize that time-out is not the only method of discipline that can reduce the following kinds of misbehavior.

## Misbehavior that Deserves Time-Out

Hitting
Temper tantrums
Hostile teasing of other children; provoking others
Sassy talk or back talk to parents and other adults
Angry screaming and screeching
Grabbing toys from another child
Throwing toys
Destroying toys
Kicking others
Biting or threatening to bite
Pulling hair

Choking others
Spitting or threatening to spit at others
Throwing dirt, rocks, or sticks at others
Mistreating or hurting pets and other animals
Obnoxious loud crying "intended" to punish parents
Slapping
Pinching
Scratching
Tattling
Doing dangerous things such as riding a tricycle into
  the street
Whining loudly
Hitting others with an object
Threatening by word or gesture to hit or hurt others
Cursing and swearing
Pushing others standing on a stairway
Throwing food at the dinner table
Purposefully damaging furniture or the house
Mocking or trying to humiliate parents
Loud complaining or demanding behavior, after a
  warning
Name-calling and making faces at others
Persistently interrupting adult conversation, after a
  warning
Disobeying a command to immediately stop a
  particular misbehavior

In looking over this shopping list of bad behavior, do
you recognize any part of your child's behavior you
wish to eliminate? Parents who have used the time-out
method have been able to reduce or eliminate each of
the above activities. Whether you consider a behavior
bad or bad enough to deserve time-out depends on your
values and on the goals you and your spouse have for
your child.

However, time-out is not the solution for all problem
behavior of children. Time-out should not be used for
the following behavior problems.

# Do Not Use Time-Out
# for These Problem Behaviors

Pouting, sulking
Irritableness, bad moods, grumpiness
Failing or forgetting to do chores
Failing to pick up clothes and toys
Not doing homework or piano practice
Overactive behavior (but do time-out aggressive or
  destructive acts)
Fearfulness
Being dependent, timid, or passive
Reclusiveness, wanting to be alone
Behavior not observed by the parent


Use other forms of child management to help with these kinds of problem behavior. Time-out is not effective when used on some problem behavior. Actively ignore quiet pouting, soft crying, and whimpering (Chapter 3).

Parents often ask if they can use time-out to get their child to start doing something fairly complex such as, "Straighten your room" or "Do your homework." Time-out is effective in *stopping* bad behavior. Threatening your child with time-out doesn't encourage him to begin a chore which is both complex and distasteful. To get your child to do a distasteful chore, consider using Grandma's Rule (Chapter 3), token rewards (Chapter 10), or, for the older child, a parent-child contract (Chapter 10).

When you press your child to do a disagreeable chore, he might sass you or have a temper tantrum. Do use time-out on this back talk or temper tantrum. Once you stop this interfering behavior, it will be easier to get your child to do distasteful chores. Be sure to praise his efforts to begin and complete unpleasant tasks.

# SELECT ONLY ONE OR TWO KINDS OF TARGET BEHAVIOR

You and your spouse need to select one or two kinds of bad behavior for which to begin the time-out method. This behavior is called the target behavior, because your aim or goal is to change it. Use time-out consistently and repeatedly on a target behavior.

Don't begin using time-out on all of your child's inappropriate or unacceptable behaviors; he might spend all day in time-out! After gaining success in decreasing the first target behavior, you can select another target behavior to be decreased.

How do you go about selecting a target behavior? Look over the list of misbehaviors that deserve time-out and choose one of these or a similar misbehavior. The behavior should be countable: for example, you should be able to actually count the number of times that your child sasses you or tattles on a brother or sister.

Also, be sure that the target behavior you select occurs frequently. You won't be able to obtain adequate experience in learning how to use time-out unless the behavior occurs at least once a day.

When first beginning the time-out method, you might select two kinds of target behavior, one minor problem behavior and one major problem behavior. Begin using time-out with a minor target behavior such as tattling or teasing. These are easy target behaviors to handle, because children are usually not extremely emotional or angry when tattling or teasing.

Later, after getting experience in using time-out, move on to a major target behavior such as hitting or temper tantrums. These misbehaviors are usually more challenging, since children are more emotional or angry when demonstrating these behaviors.

Use time-out repeatedly on the target behavior. When first using time-out, use it each time the target behavior occurs. You should see a 50 to 90 percent decrease in the target behavior within one or two weeks.

## COUNT HOW OFTEN THE TARGET BEHAVIOR OCCURS

Before you begin using time-out, it's a good idea to actually count and record how often the target behavior occurs. Then, after you have been using time-out for awhile, you can see how much the misbehavior has decreased.

Some parents place tally marks on a wall calendar, a convenient place to keep a record of the target behavior. For example, one mother put a mark on the calendar each time her daughter tattled. Mother didn't bother keeping track of "tattles" all day long—just the tattles that occurred each day from supper time to bedtime.

A curious thing sometimes occurs if a child sees his parent record tally marks. Often the child's target behavior abruptly decreases without the parent even using time-out.

You may think it's a nuisance to keep a record of target behavior. However, this record will tell you how effective you have been in reducing your child's misbehavior.

The following example of Cindy shows how one mother began using time-out to greatly reduce her daughter's persistent "sassy talk."

### "TIME-OUT FOR SASSY TALK"

Cindy was an attractive five-year-old with blue eyes and long, blonde hair. She was bright, assertive, verbal with adults and children, and generally lovable.

However, Cindy had one bad habit. Cindy was sassy. Cindy was sassy whenever she felt like it. She usually felt like being sassy whenever someone tried to make her do something she didn't want to do. She was sassy with her parents, her grandparents, relatives, and with other children. Even the baby-sitter complained to Cindy's parents.

Cindy controlled her parents by being sassy to them. She made them feel helpless and angry. And when others were present, her parents felt embarrassed. When Mr. and Mrs. Miller scolded Cindy for being sassy, she increased her sassy talk. Her behavior was getting worse.

Mr. and Mrs. Miller had heard about the time-out method of discipline and decided to use this method to help their daughter. Sassy talk was the "target" behavior. They were in their fourth day of using time-out, and Cindy already had been placed in time-out eight times.

Cindy's mother was busy cooking and was getting ready to set the table for supper. Cindy was busy coloring on the same table. Carrying a stack of plates, Mother said, "Please pick up your crayons and coloring books so I can set the table." Cindy ignored her mother's request and continued coloring. Again her mother stated, "Cindy, pick up your crayons and books, and do it now!" Cindy responded, "I'm not through coloring yet, *dumb-dumb!*" Cindy's mother immediately said, "Time-out! That was sassy. Time-out in the bathroom." Pouting, Cindy got down from the table and marched off to the bathroom. Cindy's mother picked up the portable timer, set it for five minutes, and placed it outside the bathroom door.

Five minutes later the timer rang. When Cindy came into the kitchen, Mrs. Miller said, "Cindy, why did you have to go to time-out?" Cindy replied, "I talked sassy to you." Mother responded, "Yes, talking sassy put you in time-out." Mother then continued setting the table.

Good for Cindy's mother! She effectively followed the basic steps of the time-out method. After the target behavior (sassy talk) occurred, she swiftly placed her daughter in time-out, set the timer for five minutes, and put it near the time-out place. She didn't spank, scold, or yell at Cindy. Instead, she simply placed Cindy in time-out. As a consequence of her sassy talk, Cindy experienced a number of immediate but brief losses. She lost the use of her crayons and her mother's attention. She also lost the ability to control her mother by talking sassy to her.

In the coming weeks, and with the repeated use of time-out, Cindy greatly decreased her sassy talk. She found improved ways of talking to her mother and to other adults.


## BASIC STEPS FOR TIME-OUT

Before you begin the time-out method, be sure you frequently reward your child's good behavior. Also, avoid unintentionally rewarding the behavior on which you plan to use time-out.

Select a target behavior on which to use time-out. Use time-out on this target behavior each time it occurs and not just when you are angry. There should be a major reduction in this target behavior within one or two weeks if you correctly follow the basic steps for using time-out.

Don't start using time-out, however, until after you have read Chapters 5 through 8. These chapters describe each step of the time-out method and give examples. Also, the instructions in these chapters are tailored for the age of your child.

Chapter 8 describes mistakes which parents often make when using time-out. You'll want to avoid making these common mistakes. Chapter 8 also discusses behavior problems parents occasionally face when first using time-out and how to handle them easily.

## BASIC STEPS FOR INITIALLY USING TIME-OUT—PARENTS' CHECKLIST

✓
_____    **Steps to follow:**

_____    1. Select one target behavior for which to use time-out.

_____    2. Count how often this target behavior occurs.*

_____    3. Pick out a boring place for time-out.

_____    4. Explain time-out to your child.

_____    5. Wait patiently for the target behavior to occur.

### TARGET BEHAVIOR OCCURS!

_____    6. Place your child in the time-out place and use no more than ten words and ten seconds.

_____    7. Get the portable timer, set it to ring one minute for each year of your child's age, and place it within hearing distance of your child.

_____    8. Wait for the timer to ring—remove all attention from your child while he or she waits for the timer to ring.

_____    9. Ask your child, after the timer rings, why he or she was sent to time-out.

*This step is important but not essential.

# MAIN POINTS TO REMEMBER

- Select one or two undesirable target behaviors to be decreased.
- Send your child to time-out using no more than ten words and ten seconds after the target behavior occurs.
- Time-out lasts one minute for each year of your child's age.
- Always use a portable timer that can ring.
- The steps for using time-out are described in Chapters 5 through 8.

# 6
# Selecting a Boring Place and Explaining Time-Out

An ideal spot for time-out is a dull place or room where your child doesn't receive any attention from you or other family members. Your child should be able to get there quickly, preferably within ten seconds.

What is the best place in your home for time-out? Look over the rooms and areas in your home and select a place that is boring for a child—a place where there is nothing interesting to see or do.

The place you select depends on your child's age. A time-out chair is best for a child between two and four years old. A child between five and twelve should be in a separate time-out room, preferably the bathroom. Since you will use time-out again and again, try a couple of different places and see which one is most effective.

## Features of Effective Time-Out Places

- Dull and boring for a child
- No people; secluded from other family members (For

safety, keep very young children within continual eye sight.)
- Clear of toys, games, television, stereo, books, pets, and interesting objects
- Safe, well-lighted, and not frightening
- Can easily get there within ten seconds

# EFFECTIVE TIME-OUT PLACES
## Time-Out Places for Two- to Four-Year-Olds
### JIMMY AND THE TIME-OUT CHAIR

Three-year-old Jimmy was getting very impatient with his mother. He had been playing quietly with his toy cars for almost fifteen minutes! He wanted his mother's attention, but she was sitting at the kitchen table drinking coffee with a neighbor.

Carrying a big toy truck to his mother he said, "You have to play with me." His mother replied, "Jimmy, when Mrs. Barton and I are finished talking, I will play with you." "No, play now!" Jimmy commanded. He then raised the truck and brought it down on his mother's knee. "Ouch! Time-out for hitting!" she responded.

Immediately, she carried Jimmy to a large straight-back chair across the room. Then she set a kitchen timer for three minutes and placed it on the floor several feet from Jimmy's chair. Jimmy began to cry, scream, and carry on.

She explained to her startled neighbor, "I've had a lot of trouble with Jimmy hitting me when he doesn't get his way. He used to hit me or try to hit me several times a day. Then I started using a time-out chair for hitting. This is the first time he's hit me in more than two weeks. His behavior isn't perfect, but that time-out chair is really helping him to control his hitting."

If your child is between two and four years of age, an ideal place for time-out is a large, straight-back chair.

It's safer than using a separate room for time-out. A large chair is dull and boring, quickly available, and limits your child's activity and movement. In addition, it's difficult for your child to quickly get down from a large chair. Never use a rocking chair, a small child's chair, the sofa, an easy chair, a playpen, or your child's bed for a time-out place.

You may place the time-out chair in the room with you, in the adjoining room, or in the hall. For your child's safety, you need to keep an eye on her, but only from the corner of your eye. Don't actually make direct eye contact with your child. You want her to feel that you are ignoring her during the brief time-out. Don't let her catch you looking at her. One way to avoid giving attention to your child is to pretend to read a magazine or newspaper.

Quickly lift your toddler onto the time-out chair. Next, place the ticking timer several feet from the time-out chair. After the timer rings, lift your child down from the chair or tell her that she may get down. In Chapter 8, we'll discuss what to do if you think your child might not stay in time-out.

Let your child sit or kneel on the chair, but not stand or jump or touch her foot to the floor. Some children have tantrums on the chair. Consequently, it shouldn't be placed within kicking or hitting range of the wall or near dangerous or valuable objects. If you think your child might fall off of the chair, place the chair over a rug.

Parents sometimes place the time-out chair in a corner of the room, turn it to the wall, and make their child face the wall. You may place the chair in a corner. However, don't demand that your toddler or pre-schooler face the wall or corner. Requiring that your child face the wall is overly harsh. Also, it would take constant effort on your part to make the child face only one direction and unintentionally gives her a lot of your attention. Let your child face whatever direction she wants to face. However, do require that she either sit or kneel on the chair.

Your child shouldn't take any toys, dolls, or pets to time-out and shouldn't be able to see the television set from her chair. Tell brothers and sisters not to pester or talk to her. Warn them that if they do, then they will be sent to a separate chair for time-out.

Your child will probably call out to you from her chair, asking for attention and reassurance. She may even say that you are a "bad mama" or threaten to "run away from home." Actively ignore her and don't answer or make eye contact with her. Answering or looking at her are forms of attention and reduce the effectiveness of time-out. Resist feeling guilty or miserable while she is sitting on the chair. After all, time-out lasts only two to four minutes and will soon be over.

Some parents place their preschooler directly on the floor in the corner of a quiet room or in a semi-deserted hallway rather than using a time-out chair. A particular spot on the floor can be a good place for time-out if your child has learned to stay in one place. However, point to the exact spot where she is supposed to sit.

## TIME-OUT PLACES FOR FIVE- TO TWELVE-YEAR-OLDS

Children who are between five and twelve years old should be placed in a separate room for time-out. It's safer to leave an older child alone in a time-out room than a preschooler who needs close monitoring.

Your home has several good time-out places such as a bathroom, laundry room, your bedroom, or a deserted utility room or hallway. Usually, the bathroom is the best place for time-out. This might sometimes cause an inconvenience to the rest of the family. Having a problem child, however, can cause an even bigger inconvenience to family members. At first, your child might seem to enjoy playing in the water or making paper airplanes out of facial tissue while in the bathroom. However, the child will soon get tired of this. While waiting in time-out, a child frequently claims to need to use the bathroom. Needing to use the bathroom isn't a problem if your child is already there! The bathroom is an excellent time-out place.

Before you first begin using time-out, be sure to prepare the time-out room. Besides being dull and free of interesting objects, it should also be made safe. Any objects that might be dangerous, such as glass, sharp objects, medications, or poisonous cleaning chemicals, should be removed from the room. After your child settles down and adjusts to time-out, you might return most of the objects to the room. Place the timer several feet outside the door so your child can hear it while it is ticking and when it rings.

## Never Use Your Child's Bedroom

Your child's bedroom may seem to be the most "convenient" place for time-out. However, the effectiveness of the time-out method will be severely reduced if you use your child's bedroom. A time-out place should be dull and boring with nothing interesting to do or see. A child's room usually has toys, games, a radio, stereo, or books. It's not dull and boring. Be effective when you use time-out. Resist the temptation to use your child's room as a time-out place.

After going to the time-out room, your child can do whatever she wants as long as she doesn't make a mess or destroy things. She can sit, stand, or walk around the room. If she makes a mess, by scattering objects around the room or spilling water on the floor, she must clean it up. If she damages something, she must help pay for it. Effective methods for easily handling occasional rebellious time-out behavior are discussed in Chapter 8.

# Never Use a Frightening Time-Out Place

## "DAGEON THE DRAGON!"

Several years ago I counseled Mr. and Mrs. Meyers regarding ways they could help Bennie, their five-year-old son. Bennie was energetic and difficult to handle. He often grabbed toys away from his little sister or hit her.

We decided to use time-out for hitting and for grabbing toys. Mr. and Mrs. Meyers were supposed to discuss this method between themselves but not use it until we had another appointment to discuss the correct steps. However, when we met the following week, I was shocked to learn that they had tried to frighten Bennie with time-out.

They told Bennie that if he hit his little sister or grabbed toys away from her, he would have to go to the basement for time-out. They further explained that a dragon named Dageon lived in their basement! Bennie became hysterical, promised to be good, and pleaded with his parents not to send him to the basement.

Sensing Bennie's intense fear, Mr. and Mrs. Meyers stopped threatening to put Bennie in the basement. They also told him that there was no dragon there.

Time-out should never be scary. A frightening place for time-out is likely to cause emotional problems in a child. The purpose of time-out is not to frighten a child, but to bore him.

# EXPLAINING TIME-OUT

You and your spouse have selected a target behavior to be decreased and have selected a boring place for time-out. Your next steps are to explain time-out and to wait for the target behavior to occur.

Introduce time-out when both you and your child are relaxed. Also, be sure that both you and your spouse join together in describing time-out. Your child needs to know that you both expect her to follow the rules in going to time-out and staying there until the timer rings.

Tell your child that both of you love her, but that her behavior of _____ is causing problems for her and the family. She might quietly listen or want to argue with you about time-out. Don't argue or debate whether you and your spouse have the right to put her in time-out.

## Explaining Time-Out to Two- to Four-Year-Olds

If your child is between two and four years of age, it's best to demonstrate and practice time-out in addition to explaining it.

### HELPING MELISSA TO STOP BITING

Melissa is three years old. When she gets angry with other children she both threatens to bite and actually bites. Mom, Dad, and Melissa are all sitting at the kitchen table.

MOTHER:  Melissa, your daddy and I both love you. We also want to help you. Remember yesterday when you got mad at James? You acted like you were going to bite him. Biting is against the rule.

MELISSA:  Can I have a Coke?

FATHER:  Yes, in a couple of minutes. But right now we want to talk about biting and how to help you stop biting. If you bite or pretend to bite, you must sit on a chair. And you can't get down till this timer rings. When this timer rings you may get off the chair.

MELISSA:  Can I have a Coke now?

MOTHER:  In a minute. Let me show you what happens when you bite. (Mother picks up Melissa and sets her on a large chair in the corner of the kitchen.) When Mommie puts you here, you have to stay here. You can sit or kneel on the chair, but you can't stand up. And you can't get down or you will be in big trouble! You have to sit here until the timer rings. (Father rings the timer.) Did you hear the timer ring? That means you may get down now. (Mother lifts Melissa from the chair and places her on the floor.) That is time-out.

MELISSA:    Are you going to get me a Coke now?

MOTHER:    Yes, I will get you a Coke. But you re-member—when you bite or pretend to bite someone, Mommie or Daddy will put you on a chair. You will have to stay there until the timer rings.

Obviously, Melissa wasn't paying very close attention to her parents' explanation and demonstration of time-out. Melissa's parents will explain and demonstrate time-out two more times before actually using it. They could demonstrate time-out by using one of Melissa's dolls or stuffed animals. Melissa will learn more about time-out, however, by actually experiencing it after she bites or threatens to bite.

## Explaining Time-Out to Five- to Twelve-Year-Olds

If your child is older than four years of age, you also will need to introduce time-out to her. Look at the following example of parents explaining time-out.

### TELLING TIM ABOUT TIME-OUT

Ten-year-old Tim has been hitting and threatening to hit his younger brother and other children when he gets angry with them. Other children are beginning to reject Tim because of his hitting and aggressiveness. Dad, Mom, and Tim are sitting around a small table.

FATHER:     Your mom and I want to talk with you about the problem you've been having with hitting your brother and other kids when you get mad. We both love you, and we want to help you with this problem. Hitting is causing problems for you, your brother, and the whole family.

TIM:        Bobby starts it most of the time! I just hit him back when he hits me or calls me names.

MOTHER:     Yes, sometimes Bobby hits you and calls you names. Even though he is only five years old, he still needs to behave himself. We are going to have a talk with him, too. But now let's talk about you and time-out.

FATHER:     Every time you hit or threaten to hit someone, your mom or I will say "time-out"! That means that you must go to the bathroom immediately and stay there for ten minutes. We will set this timer for ten minutes. When you hear it ring, you may come out. You can't come out until it rings. If you don't go to time-out immediately or if you make a lot of noise in time-out, then you get extra minutes added on the timer. If you make a mess in time-out, then you get extra minutes on the timer and you have to clean up the mess before you come out.

TIM:        Who invented time-out anyway? What happens if I don't go to time-out? What happens if I leave time-out when I get ready?

MOTHER:     Your dad and I expect you to go to time-out and stay there till the timer rings. If you don't go, then no television and no bicycle for the rest of the day, until you go to time-out. Then you have to stay in time-out for ten minutes plus one extra minute for every minute you delay going. You might have to stay as long as fifteen minutes if you don't go right away or if you leave time-out before the timer rings. When your dad and I tell you to go to time-out, you must go! Your job is to go and stay there till the timer rings. Tim, do you have any questions about time-out?

TIM:  Time-out is for little kids. It sounds silly. It sounds mean! Just spank me when I hit! And spank Bobby too. Will Bobby have to go to time-out?

FATHER:  If you hit each other, then you both have to go to time-out in separate places. Time-out will help you stop hitting.

MOTHER:  We love you and Bobby. We expect both of you to mind us. And when we tell you to go to time-out, you must go immediately.

When you tell your child about time-out, don't expect him to be enthusiastic about the plan. The next step for Tim's parents is to wait for the target behavior (hitting or threatening to hit) to occur.

When first beginning the time-out method, you might wonder if your child will cooperate by going to time-out and by staying there until the timer rings. An uncooperative response to time-out usually isn't much of a problem. Chapter 8, however, tells you what to do if you think your child might rebel against time-out.

## MAIN POINTS TO REMEMBER

- Use a large straight-back chair as a time-out place for children between two and four years of age.
- Use a separate time-out room for children between five and twelve years of age.
- Never use your child's bedroom as a time-out place.
- You and your spouse both need to describe time-out to your child.

# 7
# Quickly Getting Your Child to Time-Out

This chapter will teach you the exact steps to follow in placing your child in time-out. It's important to get there quickly. Getting to time-out swiftly will reduce your child's resistance and will increase the effectiveness of this method of discipline. You want your child to see an immediate connection between his bad behavior and the distasteful experience of time-out.

By now, you have selected a boring place for time-out, explained time-out, and waited for the target behavior to occur. After your son or daughter displays the undesirable target behavior, follow the basic steps described in the box, "Four Steps for Using Time-Out After the Target Behavior Occurs."

Follow these basic steps if your child is between the ages of two and twelve years. You may need to practice and gain experience before automatically following the steps. Many parents have a natural tendency to scold their child before placing him in time-out; this is a mistake. Scolding, arguing, and talking to a child before placing him in time-out encourages him to argue, become emotionally upset, and delay getting to time-out.

---

**FOUR STEPS FOR USING TIME-OUT
AFTER THE TARGET BEHAVIOR OCCURS**

1. Send or place your child in time-out and use no more than ten words and ten seconds.

2. Get the portable timer, set it to ring one minute for each year of your child's age, and place it within hearing distance of your child.

3. Wait for the timer to ring—don't give your child any attention while he or she waits.

4. Ask your child, after the timer rings, why he or she was sent to time-out.

---

Your child might try to avoid time-out by attempting to manipulate you. Children often protest, negotiate, blame another child, ask forgiveness, act indifferent, cry, plead, have a tantrum, or do something else to discourage you from sending them to time-out. Ignore all your child's remarks and displays of emotion. Remain calm and immediately place him in time-out. If he wants to talk with you, he may do so after time-out. Be easy on yourself and your child; send him to time-out quickly. Use no more than ten words and ten seconds in doing so. You'll find that time-out gets easier and easier when you use it correctly.

# GETTING YOUR CHILD TO TIME-OUT
## Getting Your Two- to Four-Year-Olds to Time-Out

### "FOR SPITTING YOU GET TIME-OUT!"
Three-year-old Amanda was developing a bad habit of spitting or threatening to spit when angry with other

children. Struggling with her sister over a toy, Amanda again introduced her effective weapon—spitting.

Mother immediately said, "For spitting you get time-out!" Quickly, Mother picked up Amanda from behind, walked across the room with her, and set her on a large straight-back chair. Amanda said, "I don't want to go to time-out! I won't do it again! . . ." Unimpressed with her daughter's promise to stop spitting, Mother made no reply and simply left Amanda sitting on the time-out chair.

Good for Amanda's mother! She correctly followed the basic steps for placing her daughter in time-out. Carry two- and three-year-old children to the time-out chair. They are too young to quickly get there on their own. Some toddlers kick when carried to time-out, so be sure to carry them from behind. You can physically guide a four-year-old as he walks to a time-out chair. Never try to comfort or be affectionate with a child while you are taking him to time-out. Be stern or matter-of-fact and tell your child, in ten words or less, why he is being placed in time-out.

## Five- to Twelve-Year-Olds

Older children who are sent to time-out must travel there on their own. Develop the habit of giving effective commands when sending your child to time-out. When your child demonstrates the target behavior, walk near him, maintain a stern facial expression, and establish eye contact. Give a direct command to go to time-out and point in the direction of time-out. Place the timer outside the door of the time-out room after your child arrives there.

Say only two things when placing your child in time-out. First, label the misbehavior your child has demonstrated or state the rule he broke. Say, "That was back talk!" or "Hitting is against the rule!" Second, command your child to go to time-out. Say, "Go to time-out!" or "Go to time-out, immediately!" Say nothing else. Now might be a good time to review the section in Chapter 2 on "How to Give Effective Commands."

Most children between the ages of five and twelve years learn to obey a clear command to go to time-out. If you think your child may refuse to go, study Chapter 8—"Common Mistakes and Problems Using Time-Out." Chapter 8 will tell you how to handle any problems.

The basic steps of using the time-out method are always the same regardless of what your child did to deserve time-out. To become effective at using time-out, follow the basic rules described in this book and gain experience by actually using this method.

When beginning the time-out method, it will be helpful to occasionally review various chapters of this book. Also, it will be helpful to discuss your time-out experiences and your child's reactions with your spouse or with another person who is interested in your child.

After placing your child in time-out, set the timer one minute for each year of your child's age, and place it within hearing distance of your child. He must wait until he hears the timer ring before leaving time-out. Don't give your child any attention while the timer is ticking.

## DETERMINING THE LENGTH OF TIME-OUT

Your child's age will determine the length of time she spends in time-out. In Chapter 5, you learned that children are to spend one minute in time-out for each year of age. If your child is two years old, always set the timer for two minutes each time you place her in time-out. If she is twelve years old, set the timer for twelve minutes. *Don't place your child in time-out for longer than one minute for each year of age!*

Some parents who mistakenly use both long and short periods of time-out find that the shorter periods of time-out become less effective. Do not use longer periods of time-out some times and shorter periods at other times. Parents often make the mistake of letting their anger toward their child's bad behavior determine how long their child will spend in time-out. Don't do this! Always use one minute for each year of age when placing your child in time-out. Only if your child rebels against time-out should she spend more minutes in time-out than usual. Handling your child's possible resistance to time-out is discussed in Chapter 8.

## ALWAYS USE A PORTABLE TIMER

Place the timer out of reach, but within hearing distance of your child—about five to ten feet from the time-out place. The floor is a good spot for a timer. Your child will learn to listen for the timer to signal when time-out is over. He will learn to depend on the timer rather than on your telling him when he may leave time-out. It's all right, but not necessary, that your child see the face of the timer. However, your child should be able to hear it ticking and when it rings. Of course, never let your child handle or play with a timer while he is in time-out.

Toddlers and preschoolers, when they are not in time-out, often enjoy playing with a timer. Sometimes they put their dolls and toy animals on a time-out chair, next to a ticking timer. Allow them to practice their time-out skills because someday they, too, will be parents!

A timer helps a parent to be consistent, organized, and fair in using the time-out method of discipline. Place the portable timer near your child after placing him in time-out. *Do not use the timer on your kitchen stove.* You will always need to bring the timer to the time-out place. Your child must be able to hear the timer ring. The timer, not the parent, determines when the child gets out of time-out. A portable timer helps remove the time-out power struggle between you and your child. *Always use a portable timer.*

### More Reasons for Using a Portable Timer:
- Timers can't be pestered and manipulated into ringing early.
- A timer doesn't forget to release a child from time-out. Parents sometimes do forget about a child in time-out.
- Your child learns to take responsibility for leaving time-out at the proper time.
- A ticking timer is a sign to other family members that a child is in time-out. Anyone giving attention to a child in time-out also runs the risk of being placed in time-out.
- When a timer is used, children stop asking parents when they may come out of time-out. Parents get more peace and time to themselves while their child is waiting for the timer to ring. Timers are parent savers.

## WHAT YOU DO DURING TIME-OUT

Remember that your main objective after placing your child in time-out is to avoid giving her any attention. Most parents need to remain in the same room when their two- or three-year-old is in time-out. After placing your toddler or preschooler on the time-out chair, command her to stay there, and say nothing else. Turn your head away from her and avoid eye contact. If a preschooler has a tantrum on the time-out chair, some parents pretend to look at a newspaper or magazine in order to avoid giving their child any attention. Your child will recognize that you are ignoring her when she is in time-out.

If your child is between five and twelve years old, he will be in a separate room for time-out, and you will have some time by yourself. Think about the steps you used in placing your child in time-out. Did you follow the basic rules and steps? If your spouse or another person who cares for your child is present, this might be a good time to discuss your child's behavior and your skill in using the time-out method. However, your child shouldn't hear such a discussion, because it might be annoying to him and encourage him to rebel against time-out.

The parents of ten-year-old Justin asked him why he often screamed and became so emotional while in time-out. He replied, "It feels good to let it all out . . . and I want you to feel as mad as I feel!" Time-out was effective with Justin, but his parents sometimes had to give each other lots of emotional support during his time-outs.

When using time-out or any method of discipline, many parents begin to feel guilty, inadequate as parents, sorry for their child, or fear losing their child's love. Recognize that these feelings are natural for a parent and that all of us have doubts about our competence as parents. However, don't let these feelings prevent you from helping your child to improve her behavior. When you begin to seriously doubt yourself and feel significantly upset after disciplining your child, turn to Chapter 1 and read the section on "Reasons Parents Don't Discipline."

If your child rebels against the time-out method, you need to study "Common Mistakes Parents Make with Time-Out," and "If Your Child Rebels Against Time-Out" in Chapter 8. These two sections will help you effectively handle your child's possible uncooperative response to the time-out method.

After the timer rings and time-out is over, what should you do or say to your child? Read on. The next section describes what you are to say after time-out is over. The final section discusses the appropriate time to decide if additional punishment besides time-out is needed.

# TALKING WITH YOUR CHILD— AFTER TIME-OUT

## A TALK WITH THOMAS—AFTER TIME-OUT

Mother was reading her book when the timer near the bathroom rang. Seven-year-old Thomas had been in time-out for mistreating his puppy. With timer in hand, Thomas walks up to his mother.

MOTHER: Hello, Thomas. Tell me, why did you have to go to time-out?

THOMAS: I had to go to time-out because I hurt our puppy.... Can I go out and play now? I want to ride my bike down to Mike's house.

MOTHER: Yes, hurting the puppy is why you went to time-out. If you want to go to Mike's house, that's fine. Be back in about an hour, though.

THOMAS: Okay, see you in about an hour. Good-bye.

Mother correctly handled this brief "after-time-out" discussion.

After your child hears the timer ring and leaves time-out, she should come to you. Your child should tell you what she did or the rule she broke that caused her to be sent to time-out. Some parents also have their child bring the timer as well.

If she tells you the correct reason for being placed in time-out, acknowledge what she says with something like, "Yes, _____ was why you had to go to time-out." That is all you should say. Normally, you shouldn't scold, make her say she is sorry, or have her promise to be good. Your child is free to go, and usually neither of you will continue to be irritated.

If she doesn't remember why she was placed in time-out or gives you an incorrect reason, then you tell her why she was sent to time-out. After telling the child the reason, say to her, "Okay, I am going to ask you again. Tell me, why did you have to go to time-out?" Continue this discussion until she can verbalize why you sent her to time-out. When this "after-time-out" discussion is over, your child is free to go.

If your child is two or three years old, use the following plan when the timer rings. Say to him, "The timer rang, you may get down now!" Tell him, in a couple of words, the reason why he was placed in time-out. Ask him to repeat the reason. Then lift him from the chair and place him on the floor. Tell him he may go and play.

If your child is four years old, he will quickly learn to get off the chair by himself after hearing the timer ring. He also should tell you why he was placed in time-out.

In the after-time-out discussion, parents sometimes learn that their child was actually "innocent" and didn't deserve to be put in time-out. When this happens to you, be sure to quickly apologize.

Having a child state why she had to go to time-out is an optional step, especially for children between nine and twelve. If your child usually wants to argue with you in the after-time-out discussion, skip this step.

If your child remains annoyed after leaving time-out, ignore her annoyance. She has a right to these feelings. If she wants to talk about whether she should have been sent to time-out, listen. Avoid arguing, however.

## DECIDING WHETHER ADDITIONAL DISCIPLINE IS NEEDED

Time-out immediately separates you and your child and gives both of you an opportunity to calm down. When used alone, time-out is normally enough punishment for bad behavior. You can avoid yelling, scolding, making ineffective threats, and getting upset. You have used one of the most effective methods for stopping bad behavior you could possibly use.

You may think that time-out is not sufficient punishment for a particular bad behavior. Perhaps another method of discipline should be used. You should consider an additional method of discipline only after you have an opportunity to calm down. The time to make this decision is while your child is in time-out. Never announce an additional punishment before placing your child in time-out.

You may decide to use scolding, a natural or logical consequence, or behavior penalty in addition to time-out. These effective methods of mild discipline are discussed in Chapter 4. Usually, after your child is in time-out and you have a chance to cool off, you'll decide that time-out used alone is sufficient. However, the correct time to decide whether you need to use additional discipline is after placing your child in time-out.

## MAIN POINTS TO REMEMBER

- Place your child in time-out quickly following the bad behavior—using no more than ten words and ten seconds.
- The length of time-out lasts one minute for each year of age.
- Always use a portable timer.
- Ignore your child until the timer rings.
- Children between two and eight years old should tell their parents why they were sent to time-out.

# 8
# Common Mistakes and Problems Using Time-Out

## QUESTIONS PARENTS ASK
## ABOUT TIME-OUT

- "What mistakes might I make using time-out?"
- "What if my child won't go to time-out?"
- "What if my child won't stay in time-out?"
- "What if my child cries and makes noise while in time-out?"

The time-out method is easy to use, but it's also easy to make mistakes. This chapter describes common mistakes parents make when using time-out. These mistakes reduce the effectiveness of time-out in changing your child's misbehavior. Making these mistakes will also cause your child to rebel against time-out. Be sure you aren't making any of these mistakes. The last sections will tell you what to do if your child tries to rebel against time-out by refusing to go to or stay in time-out.

# COMMON MISTAKES PARENTS MAKE WITH TIME-OUT

▶ **Talking or arguing with your child after placing her in time-out.**
Correct Way: Ignore your child during time-out.

▶ **Talking or arguing with your child before placing her in time-out.**
Correct Way: Use no more than ten words and ten seconds in quickly getting your child to time-out.

▶ **Using a small child's chair, rocking chair, bed, playpen, or couch as a time-out place for your toddler or preschooler.**
Correct Way: Use a large straight-back chair as a time-out place for your toddler or preschooler.

▶ **Using your child's bedroom or an interesting place for time-out with older children.**
Correct Way: Use the bathroom or another boring place for time-out with your older child.

▶ **Keeping track of the time yourself or using a timer on the kitchen stove.**
Correct Way: Always use a portable timer—and place it out of reach, but within hearing of your child.

▶ **Making your child apologize or promise to be good after she leaves time-out.**
Correct Way: After leaving time-out, your child should tell you the reason he was sent to time-out; if he doesn't remember, you tell him what he did.

▶ **Threatening to use time-out instead of using it.**
Correct Way: Actually use time-out each time the target behavior appears; don't just threaten to use it.

▶ **Trying to shame or frighten your child with time-out.**
Correct Way: Use time-out to bore your child, not to shame or frighten her.

▶ **Using very long, very short, or different periods of time for time-out.**
Correct Way: Time-out lasts one minute for each year of age.

# IF YOUR CHILD
# REBELS AGAINST TIME-OUT

Read the following sections if you are concerned about your child possibly rebelling against time-out. If she resists time-out, select and follow a plan suited both to her age and to her particular type of rebellious behavior. However, first be sure that you aren't making any mistakes using time-out.

Should your child resist time-out, you can manage this problem! Most children don't rebel beyond the first couple of weeks if their parents use time-out correctly.

Your child may be clearly angry and upset when placed in time-out. Remember, he has several purposes for displaying anger and rebellious behavior. He wants to get your attention, to punish you for placing him in time-out, and to force you to stop using time-out. Resist your child's attempts to discourage you from being an effective parent!

You have two major goals for using time-out. Your immediate goal is to abruptly stop your child's undesirable target behavior. Your long-term goal is to help your child to develop greater self-discipline and self-control. Time-out is effective in helping your child achieve these goals.

You love your child and naturally become upset when she is unhappy. Consequently, you and your spouse need to give help and emotional support to each other if your child becomes unhappy and hard to handle after being placed in time-out.

Parents should take specific steps to manage their child's resistance to time-out. If your child is between two and four years old, select a plan from the first half of this section to handle his rebellious behavior. If he is between five and twelve years of age, select a plan from the last half of this section.

## Ways Two- to Four-Year-Olds Rebel Against Time-Out

▶ **Delaying or refusing to go to time-out.**
**Plan:** Quickly carry toddlers and preschoolers to the time-out chair, even those who don't resist going to time-out. Most four-year-olds will eventually learn to walk to time-out on their own.

▶ **Making noise in time-out.** Your child may call out to you, cry, or have a tantrum on the time-out chair.
**Plan A:** Ignore your child. Turn away and avoid eye contact while she is in time-out. Noise-making in time-out will usually decrease by itself if you consistently ignore it.
**Plan B:** If your child is three or four years old, tell him that if he continues making noise you'll add minutes on the timer. If he is noisy when the timer rings, set the timer for one or two extra minutes.
**Comments:** Noise-making is usually the only type of rebellious behavior that may continue for several weeks or longer. Recognize that your child is trying to force you to stop using time-out by making noise in time-out.

▶ **"Escaping" from the time-out chair.** Your child steps down from the large straight-back chair and runs off.
**Plan A:** Retrieve your child and place her back on the chair. Stand next to the chair and harshly command her to stay on the chair. Say, "Don't you dare get off that chair!" If she continues trying to escape, consider the following alternative plans.
**Plan B:** Place your hand firmly on his leg or shoulder and look away from him. Command him to stay on the chair. Say nothing else.
**Plan C:** Stand behind the time-out chair and firmly

hold your child on the chair. Tell him that he will be released when he stops trying to get away. Say nothing else. Before beginning this method, you must be determined to win this power struggle.

**Plan D:** Firmly hold your child in your lap and sit in the chair yourself. Tell your child that you will start the timer after she stops trying to get away. You must be determined to win before beginning this method.

**Plan E:** This plan involves spanking your child if she leaves the time-out chair. Don't use this plan if you have trouble controlling your anger while disciplining.

If your child leaves the chair, bring her back and say, "If you get off the chair again, I will spank you." The next time she leaves, return her to the chair and give two (and only two) spanks on her bottom with an open hand. Then tell her, "If you get off the chair again, I will spank you again." If she leaves again, return her to the chair and give only two spanks on her bottom with an open hand. Repeat this procedure only once more. Never use this procedure more than three times and always use an open hand to spank.

**Comments:** If the above plans are not effective, you will need to consult a family counselor. Refer to Appendix C, "When and How to Get Professional Help."

Most children will stay on a time-out chair when commanded to do so. When escaping from time-out is a problem, most parents find that this problem rarely lasts more than one or two weeks after beginning the time-out method. Always use a large straight-back chair and a portable timer.

▶ **Not leaving time-out after the timer rings.**
**Plan:** Tell your child that the timer rang and that it's okay to get off the chair. Then use active ignoring or leave the room.

▶ **After leaving the time-out chair, your child continues to cry or scream.**
**Plan:** If your two- or three-year-old child continues to

scream or cry loudly after leaving time-out, walk out of the room and don't give him any attention. If your four-year-old child continues to cry loudly after leaving time-out, place her back in time-out for another four minutes. Do this only once.

▶ **After leaving time-out, your child is annoyed with you, but does not cry or scream.**
**Plan:** Ignore your child's annoyance. Don't insist that he be pleasant after leaving time-out. He has a right to his own feelings.

▶ **Your child intentionally hurts herself while on the time-out chair.**
**Comments:** A child who intentionally hurts herself usually has demonstrated this same behavior at other times when disciplined. A child who hurts herself when punished has "accidentally" learned this undesirable behavior. This behavior can be changed, but you may need to work with a family counselor. A family counselor can give you specific suggestions suited to your child.

## Ways Five- to Twelve-Year-Olds Rebel Against Time-Out

▶ **Delaying or refusing to go to time-out.** Your child does not immediately go to time-out or refuses to go.
**Plan:** If your child delays or resists going to time-out, tell him that he must go immediately or he will have to spend additional minutes in time-out. For each ten seconds he delays going to time-out, add one more minute on the timer. Silently count from one to ten in order to keep track of ten seconds. Add as many as five additional minutes of time-out on the timer.

After you add five additional minutes on the timer, warn your child that he will receive a particular behavior penalty (a loss of certain privileges) if he does not immediately go to time-out. After giving this warning, silently count from one to ten. If he has not gone to time-out by the time you reach ten, announce the behavior penalty and walk off. Do not count out loud, become angry, or argue. Simply walk off. See Chapter 4 for a description and examples of behavior penalty.

Consider the following example of how a mother dealt with her ten-year-old daughter, Kelly. Kelly was attempting to avoid time-out by arguing with her mother.

Mother refused to argue and said, "Kelly, you already have ten minutes of time-out. Now you have one more minute for not going right away. That's a total of eleven minutes." (Mother paused and counted silently to ten.) "Okay, you now have eleven minutes plus one more minute and that makes twelve minutes." Kelly stopped arguing, turned, and reluctantly walked off to time-out.

If Kelly had continued to delay going to time-out, her mother would have added as many as five additional minutes to the original ten minutes. If Kelly had not gone to time-out by then, her mother would have announced that Kelly's privilege of watching television for the rest of the day was revoked—a behavior penalty. After announcing this particular penalty to Kelly, her mother would have walked off and refused to discuss the matter any longer. If Kelly had wanted to watch television that day, she first would have had to go to time-out for fifteen minutes.

**Comments:** If your child refuses to go to time-out, give him a behavior penalty. However, also permit him to go to time-out later in the day in order to remove the behavior penalty.

When you first use time-out with your child, you and your spouse should be present so that your child knows that you agree with each other. If she delays going to time-out, you might need additional practice in giving effective commands—a skill discussed in Chapter 2. Don't scold or argue with your child if he resists going to time-out. Children who resist going to time-out usually resist for only the first week or two.

▶ **Making noise in time-out.** Your child may continuously call out to you, cry loudly, stomp her feet, say she hates everyone, or have a full tantrum.

**Plan A:** Ignore your child, stay away from the time-out room, and do not try to calm her down. Don't scold, reassure, or answer your child. Be sure not to reward her noise-making by paying attention to this behavior. The best way to decrease noise-making is to use active ignoring—to withdraw all attention from your child.

**Plan B:** Add extra minutes on the timer for noise-making. If your child is noisy when the timer rings, reset the timer for two more minutes.

**Comments:** Remember that your child's purpose for making noise is to get your attention, make you angry, and force you to stop using time-out. Don't get angry or scold him for making noise, as this rewards this undesirable behavior. Simply ignore him and set extra minutes on the timer. Be sure that you're using a portable timer so that your child doesn't learn to keep calling out to you to see if it's time to come out yet.

Making noise in time-out is one type of rebellious behavior that may continue for some time. Many parents go to a distant part of their house or apartment to avoid the noise. Going to another part of the house until the noise stops is a good idea, since this reduces stress on you and also ensures that your child will receive no attention.

## TIME-OUT AT THE MOTEL

Although in a motel, Mother and Father needed to handle their six-year-old son's temper tantrum. They placed him in time-out in their motel bathroom. However, his crying was so loud and obnoxious that they had to leave their motel room. They found themselves standing on the sidewalk outdoors until their son's time-out was over. Mother and Father correctly handled their son's noise-making by actively ignoring it.

▶ **"Escaping" from the time-out room.** Your child leaves time-out before the timer rings.

**Plan:** For each ten seconds that your child is absent from the time-out room, one more minute is added to the timer, up to a maximum of five additional minutes. If she doesn't return to time-out, or is absent more than one or two minutes, she receives a behavior penalty (such as no television for the rest of the day). Refuse to get angry, announce the behavior penalty, and walk off. Don't argue with your child. Be sure to follow through with the behavior penalty you announce.

**Comments:** Escaping from time-out is usually not a problem. If it is a problem, it rarely lasts past the first two weeks.

▶ **Making a mess in the time-out room.** Your child may scatter objects about the room or spill water on the floor.

**Plan:** Be matter-of-fact and require your child to clean up the mess before she may leave the room. Don't act shocked or scold her.

**Comments:** Recognize that making a mess in time-out is just another attempt at punishing you or forcing you to stop using time-out. The day after placing his nine-year-old son in the bathroom for time-out, one father discovered that his new aerosol container of shaving cream was empty. His son apparently had emptied the entire container in the bathroom sink and rinsed the lather down the drain.

▶ **Damaging the time-out room.**

**Plan A:** Your child must clean up the room and help pay for damages. One way that he may pay for damages is to do extra chores at home. You may need to select and arrange another room for time-out, a room that is safe but less easily damaged. However, do not use your child's bedroom.

**Plan B:** You may need to meet with a family counselor for professional help to determine specific methods to help a child who loses control when disciplined.

▶ **Not leaving time-out after the timer rings or your child says she "likes" time-out.**
**Plan:** If your child doesn't leave time-out after the timer rings say, "The timer rang. You can come out now if you want to, or you can stay in there—whatever you want to do." Then turn and walk away. Say nothing else. A bright child may say that she "likes" time-out. Don't take her statement seriously. This is just another attempt at manipulating you into not using time-out.

▶ **After leaving time-out, your child continues to scream, yell, and cry.**
**Plan:** Immediately place your child back into time-out for another full period of time-out.

▶ **After leaving time-out, your child is annoyed with you, but does not cry or scream.**
**Plan:** Don't insist that your child be cheerful after leaving time-out. Ignore his annoyance. Be sure that you don't appear or act angry after time-out is over. Also, don't "apologize" for timing-out your son or daughter.

▶ **Your child intentionally hurts herself while in time-out.**
**Comments:** A child who intentionally hurts herself when angry at her parents is trying to punish them and make them feel guilty. She is attempting to manipulate her parents. This pattern of self-destructive behavior can be changed; however, you will probably need to work with a family counselor who can tailor recommendations and a plan to fit your child.

You will need professional assistance if your child physically attacks you or runs out of the house to avoid time-out. If your child refuses to go to time-out and ignores the consequent behavior penalty day after day, you may need to get professional help.

# MAIN POINTS TO REMEMBER

- Used correctly, the time-out method is effective and easy to use.
- Used incorrectly, the time-out method is less effective and difficult to use.
- Be sure that you are not making one of the common time-out mistakes.
- If your child rebels against time-out, select a plan from this chapter to effectively handle her resistance. Be sure to use a plan suited to her age.

# PART III
# MORE WAYS TO
# MANAGE YOUR
# CHILD'S PROBLEM
# BEHAVIOR

*This section examines more methods for managing problem behavior. You'll learn how to use points, tokens, and parent-child contracts to improve a variety of behaviors. Steps for timing-out two children and for placing toys in time-out are discussed.*

*We'll study skills for managing bad behavior away from home and using reflective listening. Your reflective listening skills will help your children to both express and control their feelings and emotions.*

*The final chapter looks at more childhood problems such as hyperactivity and resisting chores. The chapter also teaches additional parenting skills such as "racing the timer" and using a "resting chair."*

*Let's look at these additional ways for helping your child!*

# 9
# Managing Bad Behavior Away from Home

When you and your child are away from home does his bad behavior ever embarrass you? Are you able to handle his loud complaining or persistent demands while visiting friends or shopping together? Do you ever think to yourself, "I'll never take him anywhere again!"

There is hope for you and your child. You can correct your child's embarrassing behavior in public. Use the methods described in this chapter and be more effective and confident when you and your child visit friends and relatives, shop, and go other places together.

To be an effective parent, you need to be a well-armed parent—equipped with a variety of sound discipline skills. Parents whose only discipline skill is nagging and scolding will do a lot of that on trips away from home with their child!

Begin with the parenting skills that you have already learned. Particularly important skills and methods include frequent praise and comments on good behavior and failure to reward bad behavior. Consider occasionally using logical consequences and behavior penalty, and sometimes employing time-out or variations of time-out. Glance back over the previous chapters to review some of these parenting skills.

## VISITING THE HOMES OF FRIENDS AND RELATIVES

Prepare your child for visits away from home. Ask him to take along books to read or several small toys. Be sure that he has something interesting to do while you're talking with adults. Before leaving home, explain to your child the behavior you expect. Explain the exact misbehavior (such as back talk or angry screaming and screeching) that will result in time-out or in a particular behavior penalty (for example, no television later). If he behaves well, praise that behavior immediately or while you are returning home.

Use immediate time-out or delayed time-out to help manage misbehavior when you and your child are visiting. Before you use time-out away from home, you should be comfortable and consistent when using it in your own home and when guests are present. In addition, your child should be cooperating with the time-out method, rather than rebelling against it.

When away from home, give your children one warning before sending them to time-out or telling them that they have "chalked up" a time-out. Just like you do at home, use one minute of time-out for each year of your child's age. Consider getting a pocket-size timer for trips away from home.

At the home of relatives or friends notice any dull, boring places that you might use for time-out. Almost any place that is free of people and interesting activities will do.

Some parents successfully use the backseat of their car as a time-out place when they are away from home, especially if their child is usually noisy while in time-out. After placing your child in the backseat, you sit in the front seat or stand outside the car. Be sure to ignore her and make sure that she doesn't have any toys while in time-out.

If possible, use an immediate time-out rather than a delayed time-out. Immediate time-outs are more effective in reducing bad behavior. When you can't send your child to time-out right away, then use delayed time-out. A child should go to delayed time-out directly after returning home. Be sure that she goes to time-out immediately. Delayed time-out should only be used with children who are four years old and older.

## KATIE ALMOST CHALKS UP A DELAYED TIME-OUT

Seven-year-old Katie and her parents are visiting friends. It's after 10:00 P.M. and Father again tells Katie that it's time to go home. Katie announces that she is not ready to leave yet and she backs up her announcement with whining, tears, and angry crying.

| | |
|---|---|
| FATHER: | Katie, ten minutes ago I told you it's time to go home. Go put your shoes and coat on now! |
| KATIE: | No, I don't want to go! I want to play some more! You never let me play when I want to! You always make me go home! (Whining turns into loud crying.) |
| FATHER: | I am going to give you one warning. Stop crying and get your shoes and coat on right now—or it's time-out when you get home! |
| KATIE: | All right! You don't have to be so mean. (Katie stops crying and puts on her shoes and coat.) Can we come back next week? I want to play some more. |
| FATHER: | We had a good time tonight. Yes, maybe all of us can get together next week. |

Father was effective in handling Katie's tantrum and refusal to return home. He warned her once and told her that if she didn't mind him, he would give her a delayed time-out.

# STORES, SHOPPING MALLS, AND RESTAURANTS

When getting ready for a shopping trip, be specific when telling your child how you want him to behave. When shopping, consider his age. Be reasonable about the length of time that you expect him to "tag along" without becoming tired, whining, and misbehaving.

If your child isn't tired, but simply acts like a pest while you are in a grocery store, shopping mall, or family restaurant, consider using a variation of time-out. In *grocery stores*, a good time-out place is usually in a corner or side aisle. Point to a safe spot on the floor for your child to sit. Turn your back, pretend to look at groceries, and don't give her any attention. If she is very young, stand near her. If she is older, stand further away. But for safety's sake, always keep your child in sight.

At *shopping malls*, benches make excellent time-out places. Have your child sit on a bench. If your child is older, pick another bench for yourself. You'll both get a break from each other and an opportunity to rest. For time-out in *restaurants*, such as McDonald's, an older child can briefly sit alone at a separate table.

Most children who are in a public place will sit quietly while in time-out. However, if your child is crying loudly, select a time-out place outside the store, such as the backseat of your car. Or you may choose delayed time-out as an alternative.

## "BE QUIET OR YOU CAN'T PLAY WITH YOUR SUPERMAN SUIT!"

Twice each week my five-year-old son, Eric, accompanied my wife to the doctor's office where she got her allergy shots. Eric spent his time making noise and running in the waiting area. My wife spent her time trying to quiet him.

Finally my wife said, "Eric, you are very noisy when we are at the doctor's office. Most of the people there are sick and waiting to see the doctor. In the future, each time that you run and are noisy, you won't be allowed to play with your Superman suit for the rest of the day." Eric lost the privilege of playing with his Superman suit only one time. His favorite activity was playing with his Superman suit. After receiving this penalty, he immediately settled down. My wife rarely had difficulty with unruly behavior during their future visits to the doctor's office.

My wife was effective in reducing our son's bad behavior while they were away from home. She used the method of behavior penalty—in this case, withdrawing a favorite activity or privilege.

When your child behaves badly in public, be sure that you don't accidentally reward and consequently strengthen that bad behavior. An example of rewarding bad behavior is allowing your child to keep the candy bar he grabbed while standing in the check-out line. Quickly returning home because your child has a temper tantrum is another instance of rewarding bad behavior. However, remember that young children tire easily. Don't make the shopping trip too long.

Reward your child if she behaves while you are shopping. Give her praise or let her get a piece of gum from the gum dispenser as you leave the grocery store, but only if she has been good. Before leaving the department store, let her look at something that she had wanted to see, such as the animals in the pet department or the dolls in the toy department.

## IN THE CAR

A miserable experience for parents is to ride in a car with a backseat of noisy, fighting children. Help prevent bad behavior by carefully organizing the car as well as the trip. Be sure that everyone (you, too!) wears a seat belt. Wearing seat belts reduces behavior problems. Seat belts prevent children from crowding too close together and invading each other's space. The trip is not only more pleasant, but safer for everyone. On long trips, one parent might sit in the backseat to keep the children from roughhousing or annoying each other. Ask your children to select toys, books, or a game to take in the car.

Before leaving on a car trip, you can often anticipate the likelihood of misbehavior occurring. If you suspect problems, tell your children in advance that a particular consequence will occur if they misbehave in the car. Also, tell them that they will get only one warning before receiving a consequence. An appropriate consequence could be a delayed time-out or a mild behavior penalty such as stopping the car for several minutes until the misbehavior ends. Pulling the car off the road for five or ten minutes is more effective if you are traveling somewhere appealing to children—such as the beach or a park.

When a child gets a delayed time-out, he must go to time-out as soon as possible, usually as soon as you return home. However, on a long car trip, he should do his time-out as soon as you stop at a rest area along the highway. He briefly stays in the car for his time-out after the rest of the family leave the car. However, you should stay near the car.

## OUTDOOR PLAY ACTIVITIES

At the park, zoo, swimming pool, and on camping trips, it's easy to use immediate time-out to manage your child's misbehavior. Point to a safe place for your child to sit—on a park bench, on a large rock, by a tree, at the corner of the playground, or in the backseat of your car. Immediate time-out is easy to use and it's effective when you follow through with it.

One mother was amazed because immediate time-out worked so well in controlling the brat behavior of her nine-year-old son while they were at the swimming pool. After receiving two immediate time-outs, he stopped splashing and dunking younger children. His behavior toward the other children improved and his mother's relationship with the other mothers greatly improved. Previously, she had tried scolding and yelling, but these methods were completely ineffective. In fact, he made faces at her when she scolded him. She considered taking him home if he misbehaved (a logical consequence), but this would punish her too! Time-out was a mild consequence, but it was completely effective in eliminating her son's misbehavior.

If your child misbehaves near your house or apartment, it isn't necessary to have her come indoors for time-out. Have her sit some specific place such as the front steps. Place the timer within hearing distance. After the timer rings, she should return it to you.

## MAIN POINTS TO REMEMBER

- **Equip yourself with a variety of sound discipline skills and don't rely solely on scolding and nagging.**
- **Be sure to frequently reward your child's good behavior with attention and praise. Do this at home and away from home.**
- **In the homes of friends, use time-out as you do in your own home.**
- **In public places, consider using immediate time-out, delayed time-out, or behavior penalty.**

# 10
# Using Points, Tokens, and Contracts

**A POINT-REWARD PROGRAM HELPS SUSAN**

Seven-year-old Susan had several kinds of problem behavior that bothered her parents. She often left clothes, toys, and books scattered about her room. Mr. and Mrs. Madison tried letting her live in the clutter (a natural consequence), but that didn't bother Susan a bit. She seemed to enjoy the mess.

When asked to help with simple chores, Susan often complained, said that she was "too tired," or whined that "chores aren't any fun." Her parents tried nagging and scolding. However, Susan continued resisting their requests.

Although frustrated, Susan's parents began a special reward program and within two weeks Susan's behavior greatly improved. How did Mr. and Mrs. Madison help their daughter change? They used a point-reward program. Read on to see how to develop such a program.

*Material rewards* (a small toy) and *activity rewards* (going to the park) help motivate children to improve their behavior. Provide a way for your child to earn tokens, points, or check marks to purchase rewards. After earning a number of points or tokens, your child can exchange them for a particular reward that she wants.

Earning *tokens* motivates adults as well as children. If you have a job outside your home, you earn tokens (in the form of paychecks and money), which you exchange for material rewards (a pizza, new shoes) and activity rewards (going to the movies or on vacation). To help your child develop a new behavior or habit, you sometimes need to offer him more than praise and attention. Once his new behavior is well established, you can phase out and eventually discontinue this special incentive program.

Parents can use token rewards with children who are four or five years old. *Point rewards* are effective with children six to twelve years of age. *Parent-child contracts*, another type of special incentive plan, are used with children from seven or eight through adolescence. Let's look closer at these special programs.

## OFFERING POINT REWARDS
### Steps for Implementing a Point-Reward Program

Follow these steps in putting together an effective point-reward program for your child:

- Select a target behavior.
- Make a *point-reward calendar.*
- Write a *menu of rewards.*
- Keep track of the points earned and spent.
- Adjust the reward program.
- Discontinue the program.

**Select a target behavior you want improved.** You must be able to pinpoint and actually count the behavior that you want increased such as clearing the table after meals.

Describe the target behavior in positive rather than negative terms. For example, Mr. and Mrs. Madison asked Susan to "have a clean bedroom" rather than to "stop having a messy bedroom." They also listed several other activities, such as emptying the trash, regularly brushing her teeth, and so on.

**Make a *point-reward calendar*.** Write down the target behavior on this calendar. Also, write down the time when you will check to see if the behavior has occurred. Next to each target behavior, list one or more points that your child might earn for that behavior. After you prepare a calendar, post it in a conspicuous place. Most parents attach it to the refrigerator door or place it on a bulletin board.

**Write down a *menu of rewards* and post it near the point-reward calendar.** A *menu of rewards* is a list of small material rewards and activity rewards (privileges) your child desires. Ask her what she would like to work for. Susan said that she wanted to work for a comic book, a particular doll, a trip to McDonald's, and so on.

After you and your child list possible rewards, then you decide how many points each reward will "cost." You don't want the rewards to be too easy or too difficult to earn, because your child might lose enthusiasm for the program. After you gain experience using a menu of rewards, it will be easier to determine the appropriate cost for new rewards. It's best to begin a point-reward program using small rewards that don't cost your child very much (and don't cost you very much) so that he has the opportunity to frequently earn rewards.

**Keep track of the points as your child earns and spends them.** When he earns a point, record it on the calendar with enthusiasm. Give lots of praise for his good behavior and the points he earns.

Encourage him to spend his points rather than save them so that he will enjoy the program more. After he spends a point and receives a reward, place a slash mark through those points.

When your child has earned enough points to select a reward, let her purchase the reward as soon as possible. If she is as young as six or seven years, be particularly quick to help her exchange points for a reward.

**Make adjustments within the program so that it works better.** Keep the old calendars after posting new ones. By looking at these old calendars, both of you can see how much progress he has made in improving his behavior.

The calendars tell you how well your program is working. To improve the program, make clearer definitions of what she must do to earn points and add new rewards to the menu. Be sure that you give her these rewards only if she earns them. If she gets rewards without working for them, why should she work?

Some parents use fines for bad behavior—they take away points that their child has earned. However, your child might get discouraged with the program if he loses points after earning them. Combine other methods of discipline for bad behavior, such as logical consequences or time-out, with the point-reward program for good behavior. For example, Susan's parents placed her in time-out when she had a tantrum. When she had a tantrum-free day, she earned two points. Her tantrums rapidly decreased.

**Phase out the program.** Don't keep a point-reward program indefinitely, just until your child's behavior improves. Tell your child that the point rewards helped him to make improvements in his behavior and that you are proud of these improvements. Continue to praise his improved behavior and discontinue the point-reward program. Parents can phase out the program in several ways. Omit giving points when he fails to ask for them. Increase the amount of time between earning the

## SUSAN'S POINT-REWARD CALENDAR FOR IMPROVING SEVERAL BEHAVIORS

### Points Earned

| List of Good Behavior (and possible points) | S | M | T | W | T | F | S |
|---|---|---|---|---|---|---|---|
| Clean bedroom, check at 6:00 P.M. (2 points) | 0 | // | // | | | | |
| Clear dinner table (each meal, 1 point) | / | // | // | | | | |
| Empty trash by 6:00 P.M. (1 point) | / | 0 | / | | | | |
| Brush teeth (each meal, 1 point) | // | / | /// | | | | |
| Be home on time after school (2 points) | 0 | 0 | // | | | | |
| Tantrum-free day (2 points) | 0 | 0 | // | | | | |
| **Total Points Earned** | //// | //// / | //// //// //// | | | | |

---

This calendar provides a record of several kinds of behavior for one week. Post a new calendar each week.

At the end of each day, total the number of points your child has earned. Draw marks through points on the bottom line when your child spends those points.

## SAMPLE MENU OF REWARDS

### Menu of Rewards

| Reward | Cost in Points |
|---|---|
| Comic book | 4 |
| Trip to McDonald's | 12 |
| Dad plays ping-pong with me | 4 |
| Soft drink from refrigerator | 6 |
| Package of sugarless gum | 3 |
| Make popcorn | 9 |
| Staying up until 9:30 P.M. on school night | 7 |
| Trip to park | 8 |
| Ice-cream bar from freezer | 6 |
| Play cards with mother | 4 |
| Trip to get pizza | 15 |
| Small toy (less than $7.00) | 30 |

This "menu" lists various material rewards and activity rewards. It also lists how many points (or tokens) your child must pay for each reward. Post this menu next to the point-reward calendar.

points and exchanging them for rewards. Consider having a party for him since he has "graduated" from the program. Take him and the family to a special place to eat that he has chosen.

# GIVING TOKEN REWARDS

Most four- and five-year-olds prefer to earn *tokens* rather than points because they can touch and hold tokens and carry them around. Use poker chips, marbles, play money, or other small objects as tokens. Don't let your child handle or play with any tokens unless she has earned them. She will need a container, perhaps a plastic jar or cup, for her tokens. If she is four or five years old, encourage her to keep the token container in a special place so she won't lose her tokens.

You need to select a target behavior and make up a menu of rewards. Give your child tokens rather than points for his good behavior. For preschoolers, draw or cut out pictures of rewards (a toy, an ice-cream bar) for the menu of rewards. Next to the picture of each reward, draw another picture showing the number of tokens she must pay for that reward.

When the desirable target behavior occurs, give your child a token. When he has earned enough tokens, he can purchase a reward. A token-reward program is simple to operate once it's set up and after your child learns that he can exchange tokens for "goodies."

### TOKENS AND ICE-CREAM BARS

Four-year-old Ann rarely answered or came when her mother called her. Mother decided to use a token-reward program and to give Ann a token each time that Ann came when called. Ann said that she wanted to work for ice-cream bars in the freezer. Mother said that each ice-cream bar would cost five tokens.

Ann earned one or two ice-cream bars a day for a

week. Mother then slowly discontinued the token-reward program; however, Ann's improved behavior of coming when called continued.

# WRITING PARENT-CHILD CONTRACTS

### "HE'S LONELY BY HIMSELF"

"He's lonely out there all by himself," eight-year-old Paul pleaded. "He gets cold in the garage. See, he always tries to make a nest to keep warm. I want him in my room."

Mrs. Carr had been listening to these same insistent, monotonous statements from Paul for the past two weeks. She was tired of hearing Paul say that he wanted his gerbil in his room. She felt sorry because Paul and his gerbil were separated. However, she knew that she would also get tired of cleaning up after the gerbil if Paul moved it inside the house.

Paul's father suggested that the three of them write up an agreement spelling out Paul's responsibilities for keeping the gerbil's cage clean. Mr. Carr said that the contract should also state the consequences if Paul didn't keep his part of the bargain. If Paul didn't regularly clean the cage, the gerbil would be returned to the garage.

A contract was written, dated, and signed by all three family members. The Carr family discovered a new way for handling family disagreements—parent-child contracts.

A *parent-child contract* is a written agreement between you and your child. All parties join together in identifying a problem, discussing and negotiating a solution, clarifying responsibilities, signing the agreement, and following through with the agreement.

Contracts are used with children as young as seven or

eight years of age. These problem-solving tools are especially useful to families with adolescents.

Think of a problem your family has. Consider negotiating a parent-child contract to resolve it.

## Steps for Writing and Using a Parent-Child Contract

Follow these steps in writing and using a contract:

- Identify a problem.
- Negotiate a solution with your child.
- Write down the agreement.
- Sign the contract and follow it.

**Identify a problem.** Contracts usually focus on resolving a single problem concerning a family, such as Paul keeping a gerbil in his room. Contracts are successfully used to encourage children to come home promptly after school and to set a time for doing homework each day. Negotiate a contract with your child before she gets a new pet. It's important to negotiate a contract before he receives a potentially hazardous object such as a BB gun, archery equipment, or a chemistry set. The contract should state that he will temporarily lose the object if he becomes careless with it.

Contracts have been used with adolescents to encourage regular attendance at school and to set a deadline for returning home after dates. Before your child begins using the family car, negotiate and sign a contract stating her responsibilities.

See Appendix A for examples of how a written agreement between child, teacher, and parent can improve a child's school progress or adjustment at school.

**Negotiate a solution with your child.** Try to jointly agree on a solution rather than forcing one on her. The older your child, the more real power or authority you should let her have in helping to figure out a solution.

Don't impose a contract on an adolescent. If you do, she may rebel and intensify family conflict.

Be sure that your spouse stays involved throughout the negotiations. Sometimes, busy or harried husbands or wives try to shift negotiating responsibilities to their spouses. Choose a time when everyone is relatively calm. Be patient, positive, and stay focused on the actual behavior or actions you want to occur.

Before my family subscribed to cable television, we spent considerable time discussing potential problems and solutions. My wife and I were concerned that our boys would watch too much television or watch programs oriented toward sex and violence. After several weeks of negotiations, the four of us signed a contract. That contract helped prevent a lot of family disagreements.

**Write down the negotiated agreement.** The contract should state what you agree to do and what your child agrees to do. State the consequences if the parties don't comply with the agreement. Include a date when the contract ends or is to be renegotiated.

The contract should be fair to all. Everyone should be gaining something as well as giving up something. It states what each person is to do and what he or she is to receive in return. Consider the contract which Mr. and Mrs. Carr negotiated with their son, Paul.

**Sign the contract, post it, and follow through with your responsibilities.** After everyone signs the contract, post it on a bulletin board or put it where everyone can find it. If your child says that a posted contract embarrasses her in front of her friends, keep the contract in a special folder.

If your child doesn't fulfill his responsibilities, follow the consequences written into the contract. Most families who use contracts say that they're great tools for preventing and solving problems.

## COMPLETED PARENT-CHILD CONTRACT

**Contract**

I, _Paul_, agree to: *(1) Clean my gerbil's cage each Saturday. (2) Vacuum around the cage each Saturday.*

We, Mother and Father, agree to: *Allow Paul to keep the gerbil in his bedroom. If cage and surrounding area aren't cleaned each Saturday, then gerbil goes back to the garage.*

Date contract begins: *5/13/8-*

Date contract ends: *Contract continues as long as gerbil is in Paul's room.*

Date contract signed: *5/13/8-*

Agreed to by: *Paul*
(CHILD'S SIGNATURE)

*Mother*
(MOTHER)

*Father*
(FATHER)

Contracts help families by clarifying agreements and responsibilities. If Paul doesn't clean his gerbil's cage each week as agreed, then his gerbil must be returned to the garage.

# MAIN POINTS TO REMEMBER

- Point rewards and tokens can motivate your child to improve a wide variety of problem behaviors.
- Your child can select tangible rewards and privileges from a menu of rewards after earning points or tokens.
- Parent-child contracts help solve family problems, especially disagreements between parents and older children.

# 11
# Timing-Out Two Children and Timing-Out Toys

In this chapter, you'll learn why timing-out two children is an effective method for handling problems between children. You'll also learn when and how to correct misbehavior by timing-out a toy instead of your child.

## WHEN AND HOW TO USE TIME-OUT FOR TWO

### TIME-OUT FOR TWO

Ten-year-old Andrew and nine-year-old Angela were making faces and calling each other names. Since Father believed that Andrew had started the conflict, Father placed only Andrew in time-out.

As Andrew returned from time-out, Father overheard another argument beginning between Andrew and his sister.

ANGELA: You had to go to time-out, Andrew! Ha, ha, ha! Dad is on my side and he put you in time-out!

ANDREW: Shut up! You know that you started calling me names first. Do you want to get a fat lip?

ANGELA: Ha! Just try it! You are a big baby and you are always starting fights around here, and Mom and Dad know it!

At this moment Father walks up, annoyed with both children.

FATHER: Time-out for fighting! Angela, you in the bathroom! Andrew—the back bedroom! Go!

Good for Father! He recognizes that it takes two to fight. Also, he is beginning to realize that "time-out for two" often is more effective than punishing only one child or personally solving persistent problems between his children.

Time-out for two may be used with children who are at least three or four years old. Name-calling, using threatening gestures, loud arguing, hostile teasing, and hitting are common behavior problems parents face. If you act as a judge or referee, you might take too much responsibility for solving problems between your children. Too frequently, parents intervene and attempt to determine which child started the disagreement in order to blame and scold the guilty child. Consequently, the children become overly dependent on parents to settle problems rather than resolving their own problems. And the possibility always exists that the parent may judge incorrectly.

Many children delight in getting a brother or sister into trouble. A clever child may begin an argument but make it appear as if the other child started the conflict. Sometimes, a younger child who appears helpless or innocent actually provokes an older child into harassing him. When your children have disagreements and arguments, it's frequently difficult to say who started the conflict.

Children love getting attention from their parents. Your children may be learning to get considerable attention from you by constantly arguing and fussing with each other. Of course you dislike hearing and seeing conflict between your children; however, if you step in and handle the disagreement yourself, you may be accidentally rewarding one or both of your children for continuously arguing.

What should you do as a parent? When two children are arguing and fighting with each other, consider sending both children to time-out.

There are three advantages for timing-out both children. First, you don't have to take sides or determine which child is mostly at fault. Second, you don't accidentally reward them with lots of attention while you settle their arguments. Third, both children are discouraged from continuing their conflicts because both receive the same boring and unpleasant experience of time-out.

Time-out for two is effective for handling problems between two or more children as discussed above. Another appropriate time to use time-out for two is when your children get into trouble together, even though they may be getting along fine with each other. Let's assume that, despite several scoldings, your children continue chasing each other through the house, playing tag, and slamming doors. This would be a suitable time to place both children in time-out.

Look over the list, "Misbehavior that Deserves Time-Out" in Chapter 5, "Getting Started with Time-Out." Time-out for two would be fitting for almost all of these kinds of behavior if both children are involved in these activities together.

Prior to using time-out for two, you should be experienced in timing-out each of the children individually. Before actually placing two children in time-out, wait for the moment when both children are misbehaving. Then immediately tell both of them to go to time-out, but to different time-out places. Be sure that no one takes any toys to time-out and that they can't see each other from their separate time-out places. Place the timer where each child can hear it ring. (Of course, more than two children may be timed-out if each has experienced time-out on previous occasions.)

How long should the children be in time-out if they are, for example, six and ten years old? Set the timer for eight minutes, since their average age is eight.

Be sure to give your children attention and special privileges when they behave and get along with each other. One mother of two young children, after experiencing a pleasant morning at home, said, "You two are playing so well with each other this morning. Let's go to the park this afternoon! It's easy to go places together when you get along so well."

## TIMING-OUT A TOY
## INSTEAD OF YOUR CHILD

This section describes a useful variation of time-out— timing-out a toy instead of your child. It's easy to follow the correct steps for using this effective method of discipline. Other skills discussed in the last section include using a timer to take turns and placing personal belongings in a *Sunday Box* if they are left scattered about the house.

### TIMING-OUT THE ROBOT
### INSTEAD OF THE CHILDREN

Last night Father enjoyed bringing home a toy robot for five-year-old Jeffrey and six-year-old Lisa. This morning he reluctantly spent most of his time deciding who had the toy first, insisting that both children take turns, and scolding them for arguing with each other.

To stop the nearly continuous squabbling, Father

finally decided to put the toy robot in time-out. He placed the robot on top of the refrigerator, set the portable timer for ten minutes, and put the ticking timer next to the robot. He then turned to his children and said, "After the timer rings, I will get the robot down for you. If you two continue having problems sharing the toy, then it will go back into time-out!"

The robot didn't have to go back into time-out that morning because Jeffrey and Lisa learned to share their new toy rather than having it put in time-out. They each learned they would lose the fun of playing with their new toy if they continued fighting over it.

Children spend an enormous amount of time playing with toys and other objects. Toys provide a way for children to socialize with other children and with their parents. You can help children learn increased self-control and ways to share when they play with toys and with each other.

Consider *timing-out a toy* instead of using some other method of discipline. You might use this new method of discipline in several kinds of situations: your child misbehaves while playing with a toy (such as damaging furniture with a toy); two children misbehave, and their misbehavior involves a toy (playing catch with an expensive toy not intended to be thrown); and two children argue and fuss over a toy rather than sharing it.

When your child invites a friend over to play and the two children misbehave while playing with a toy, you might consider timing-out the toy. The parents of the other child couldn't object to your placing a toy in time-out—although they might be puzzled by this procedure. For adults responsible for several children at one time, such as preschool teachers and day-care workers, timing-out a toy is an ideal method of discipline.

You may be wondering why parents should time-out a toy instead of their child. The reason is that you don't want children spending too much time in time-out. A child who is in time-out loses the opportunity to learn new things and to try new behavior that might be rewarding or enjoyable. Also, when you use discipline, you should use the form that is mildest, while still being effective in changing behavior. Timing-out a toy is a milder punishment than timing-out the child. Timing-out a toy gives you an effective alternative to timing-out your child and an additional way to back up your warnings.

When two children repeatedly fuss over a toy, don't be overly concerned with finding out which child is at fault or which child should be blamed for the argument. *Avoid taking sides.* Simply place the toy or object in time-out. That way neither child will be rewarded for arguing and fussing. Also, after the two combatants lose their toy to time-out, they will be more highly motivated in the future to work out their own problems.

## STEPS FOR TIMING-OUT TOYS

What steps do you take when timing-out a toy or another object? When your child misbehaves with a toy, quickly remove the toy and place it in time-out. Use no more than ten words and ten seconds before placing the toy in time-out. After timing-out the toy, tell your child why it had to go to time-out. Then ask him to state aloud why the object was placed in time-out. Be brief and avoid scolding.

Don't require your child to place a toy in time-out himself. You can do it much quicker and also avoid a possible power struggle. Always use a portable timer. It will signal your child when she may resume playing with a toy. The reasons for using a portable timer when timing-out toys are essentially the same as for timing-out children. Review "More Reasons for Using a Portable Timer" in Chapter 7.

## TIMING-OUT TOYS AND OTHER OBJECTS— EXAMPLES FOR PARENTS

| Problem Behavior | A Solution |
| --- | --- |
| • Two sisters, ten and thirteen years old, continue squabbling with each other about which television program to watch. They repeatedly complain to Mother and want her to solve their problem. | • Mother turns off the television, sets a timer for ten minutes, and places the timer on the television set. (She should repeat the procedure if necessary.) |
| • Four-year-old Alan repeatedly rides his tricycle too near the street after being told not to do so by Father. | • Father puts the tricycle in a time-out place inside the garage for twenty minutes. |
| • Six-year-old Andrea plays "catch" with her pet hamster. | • The hamster is placed back in its cage and can't come out for the rest of the day. |
| • Daniel and his friend, both four years old, knock over each other's blocks, and threaten to throw them at each other. | • Daniel's mother sets a timer for ten minutes and places it next to the pile of building blocks. Mother also explains time-out to Daniel's surprised friend. |
| • Erin repeatedly complains that her brother won't take turns with their new video game. | • Father turns off the video game and sets the timer for ten minutes. (He may need to repeat this a couple of times.) |
| • The stereo in the living room is "vibrating" the apartment again. | • The stereo is turned off, and the portable timer is set for fifteen minutes and placed on the stereo. |

For children who are two or three years old, place the toy out of the child's reach or where you can easily observe. Next, get the portable timer and set it for a short period of time, usually two to five minutes. Place the ticking timer next to the toy so that your child sees the toy and timer together. Then briefly tell him why the toy went to time-out. For example, say, "You hit the coffee table with your toy. That is why I put your toy in time-out." Next, tell him that the toy can leave time-out as soon as the timer rings. When the timer rings, again briefly tell him why the toy had to go to time-out and then hand it to him. You shouldn't ask him to apologize for his bad behavior or make him promise to be good in the future.

For children who are four and older, it's usually not necessary to place the toy out of the child's reach. Simply say, "Time-out for (give name of object)! Don't touch it!" Get the timer, set it for ten to fifteen minutes, and place it next to the toy. Then tell your child why you placed the toy in time-out. Tell her that she may retrieve the toy from time-out after she hears the timer ring. No one touches a ticking timer or an object in time-out. If they do, then they have to go to time-out themselves. Even impulsive children quickly learn to control themselves and to wait for the timer to ring before removing a toy from time-out.

## MORE IDEAS FOR PARENTS

Help your children to practice taking turns by using a timer. Timers keep accurate track of the time and are fair to each child.

For example, if your two children have trouble sharing a new video game, sit down with them and have them practice the desirable behavior (taking turns). Have each child set the timer for five minutes and play the video game until the timer rings. Then the child playing the game immediately must give up the game and hand it to the other child. The other child sets the timer for five minutes and begins his turn.

Continue helping them to practice setting the timer and taking turns until you are sure both children know the procedure. If they choose, however, to continue squabbling over the video game rather than sharing it, place the video game in time-out. This will motivate each of them to cooperate.

It's often difficult to get children to pick up their toys, shoes, clothes, records, and other objects that they leave on the floor and scattered about the house. Use a *Sunday Box* for out-of-place personal belongings.

Place a cardboard box, marked *Sunday Box*, in the living room or in any other room you want cleared of clutter. Set a timer for ten minutes and place it next to the box. Then announce to your family that you are putting all out-of-place belongings in the box when the timer rings. The objects are kept there until Sunday, when you release them to their owners. Give no further warning and do not scold. After the timer rings, pick up all out-of-place objects, place them in the box, and place the box in a closet. No one touches the objects or the Sunday Box until Sunday. After losing their toys and other objects several times, your children will pick up their own belongings and you won't have to scold and nag.

When you see two toddlers or preschoolers arguing and fussing over a toy, consider using distraction. Draw their attention or redirect their interest to a new toy or activity. One or both children will usually give up the old toy or activity and try the new activity. Consequently, they have another opportunity to play cooperatively or apart from each other. Most young children can be easily distracted.

When your child plays well with others, reward him

with your praise, approval, and attention. Young children need lots of encouragement, and they love words of·praise for their good behavior.

## MAIN POINTS TO REMEMBER

- Since it takes two to fight, consider using time-out for two.
- Follow the same steps for timing-out two or more children as timing-out one child. Send them to separate time-out places.
- When your children's misbehavior involves a toy, consider removing the toy and placing the toy in time-out.

# 12
# Helping Your Child Express Feelings

**"NO GIRLS ALLOWED!"**

Relaxing in his easy chair, Father jumped when ten-year-old Stacy slammed the front door and entered the room. Wearing a baseball cap, glove, and an angry scowl, she said, "Next time I am going to use my bat on those boys!"

FATHER: What happened, Stacy? Tell me about it.
STACY: I went out to play ball and those mean boys wouldn't let me play!
FATHER: They wouldn't let you play?
STACY: No! They said, "No girls allowed" and then they all laughed at me!
FATHER: They said that you couldn't play with them because you are a girl? I can see why you feel hurt and angry. . . .
STACY: Yes, they made me mad! And they hurt my feelings, too. I thought they were my friends.

Father gave Stacy emotional support by being concerned, listening, and reflecting her feelings. He helped her realize that she was feeling more than just anger. She was also feeling hurt and rejected.

We like to protect our children from disappointments, frustrations, and conflicts with other people. However, we can't constantly keep them under our protective wing. What we can do is help them understand and cope with their feelings from unpleasant experiences. By reflectively listening, we encourage our children to express and share feelings with us. *Reflective listening* is briefly summarizing and restating to your child both her feelings and the situation causing those feelings.

By sharing unpleasant feelings with you, your child will be less hurt or burdened by them. She'll also gain increased control over her emotions and behavior, and will make better choices in meeting the challenges of daily living. Communication with your child will improve, and you'll have a closer relationship.

How early should parents begin reflective listening? Three-year-olds aren't too young to benefit if parents are brief and use simple words. Boys need help in expressing feelings as much as girls. Boys and girls who are in touch with their own feelings become better adjusted men and women.

## BASIC SKILLS OF REFLECTIVE LISTENING

Use the communication skill of reflective listening to help your child learn to express her feelings.

### Guidelines to Follow When Your Child Begins to Share Her Feelings with You

**Accept and respect all of your child's feelings.** Do this by listening quietly and attentively and being nonjudgmental. Of course, you needn't accept all of her actions or behavior, just her feelings. She can tell you how angry she is at her brother, but she isn't permitted to· show aggression by teasing or hitting him.

**Show her that you are listening to what she says.** Your close attention rewards her for expressing her ideas and feelings to you. Stop what you are doing, turn toward her, maintain eye contact, and listen carefully. Also, show her your attention by nodding your head and by an occasional, "Um hmm . . . yes . . . mmm. . . ."

**Tell your child what you hear her saying and what you think she is feeling.** Occasionally summarize, restate, or rephrase the core of what she tells you—both her feelings and the situation that caused her feelings. It's not enough to only listen and understand. You must also reflect back to her, with words, what she is saying, thinking, and feeling. This is reflective listening—a skill that takes practice to perfect. Try not to repeat your daughter's exact words. Use similar words that capture the same meaning and feeling. Say to your disappointed three-year-old, "You feel bad (the feeling) because you couldn't go to the store with Daddy this time (the situation)."

Your child may say things you find terribly upsetting or threatening. For example, she may say, "No one at school likes me!" Brace yourself and don't be swept away by a flood of concern or guilt as you listen and reflect what she says. Be a helpful parent and encourage her to express whatever she feels. She needs your help. By being an effective sounding board and mirror for your child, you are helping her cope with her feelings and make better choices and plans for herself.

Children often exaggerate both their negative feelings and the distasteful situation behind those feelings. Help your child understand and clarify her feelings and her description of the situation by reflective listening. However, don't tell her that she is exaggerating, because this will make her less willing to share other feelings with you.

**Give her feelings a name.** After listening carefully to what she says and watching her facial expressions, make an "educated guess" and tentatively label her feelings. For example, say to your nine-year-old, "You seem to be feeling disappointed (a feeling) or perhaps a little resentful (another feeling) because of the way your teacher treated you (the situation)." If you are incorrect with your first guess, then try again. Be respectful, calm, and maintain a slow pace in what you say. Encourage her to tell you if your guess is wrong and to help you correct your guess.

The list "Names for Unpleasant Feelings" gives labels for common negative feelings that confront children and adults. If your child is young, be sure to use simple words when you label her feelings.

**Offer advice, suggestions, reassurance, or alternative ways of looking at things, only after you help your child examine how she feels.** Advice, suggestions, and reassurance, if given first, will hamper your child's effort to express her feelings.

How do you begin learning the skill of reflective listening? The technique for reflecting positive feelings is the same as for reflecting negative feelings. Most parents find it easier and more pleasant to practice the skill of reflective listening by beginning with their child's positive feelings.

## Names for Unpleasant Feelings

Angry, mad
Resentful, want to get even
Irritable, grumpy
Scared, afraid
Disappointed, let down
Lonely, left out
Without a friend, rejected
Worthless, no good

Stupid, dumb
Upset, tense
Worried, anxious
Insecure
Unhappy, miserable
Messed over, unfair
Unloved, neglected
Discouraged
Embarrassed
Hurt
Tired
Bored
Confused
Frustrated
Inferior

The next time your child tells you something and seems to have positive feelings (such as feeling excited, relieved, eager, proud, or happy), reflect these feelings. Also, reflect his description of the situation or event that caused the feelings. For example, say, "You seem to feel relieved (the feeling) because your piano recital was cancelled (the situation)." Or say, "Getting invited to Mike's party (the situation) has sure made you feel excited and happy (the feeling)." Practice the skill of reflective listening in order to learn it.

### "I FEEL LIKE I DON'T HAVE A FRIEND ANYMORE"

When my oldest son, Eric, was four, I found him crying by his swing set. Tears were streaming down through the dirt covering his face. Sobbing, he said, "I hate Kenneth! He threw dirt in my face!" I tried to reflect his feelings by saying, "You're mad at Kenneth for throwing dirt and also he hurt your feelings." He replied, "Yes, I feel like I don't have a friend anymore!"

We walked to the house and I helped wash off the dirt. More important, I helped him cope with an insult from a friend by simply reflecting his feelings of anger and hurt. Later that afternoon, I watched Eric and Kenneth happily playing together.

## PROBLEMS PARENTS FACE WHEN USING REFLECTIVE LISTENING

Several problems may arise when your child expresses feelings to you. You can manage each of these problems!

**Your child expresses unpleasant feelings toward you.** He may say, "You won't let me go to the movies Friday night, and I'm mad at you!" Allow him to express negative feelings toward you, but don't permit him to verbally abuse you. Don't allow him to call you names, swear at you, threaten, or have a screaming tantrum. Tell him that he may express his feelings, but that you won't tolerate verbal abuse. If he continues calling you names or screaming, consider leaving the room or using mild punishment.

Children must learn to express their feelings without being aggressive, obnoxious, or verbally abusive. Also, when you express your feelings toward your child, be sure that you follow the rules too, and don't verbally abuse him. Be a good role model!

**You help your child to talk about her feelings; however, she continues feeling miserable or voices irrational plans.** Even after you have listened carefully, given her useful suggestions, and mentioned the possible consequences of her actions, twelve-year-old Laura may still be unreasonable. She may walk away saying, "My English teacher is mean and unfair and I hate her! But I'm going to show her. She'll be sorry. I'm going to keep whispering in class and I'm going to hand in my report late!" Often we can't directly change our child's irrational feelings and plans. Laura may have to learn to improve her behavior through natural consequences—

the school of hard knocks. That is, she may continue having to stay late after school for whispering in class and she may get an "F" for that late report.

**Your child is critical of your attempts at reflective listening.** Consider the following discussion between Mother and ten-year-old Bradley.

BRADLEY: I'm mad at Chad's parents. They won't let him do anything. They're always afraid he'll get hurt. They treat him like a baby.

MOTHER: You are saying that you are annoyed at his parents because they baby him?

BRADLEY: That's what I said! There you go again, repeating what I say!

MOTHER: Well, Bradley, I am interested in your thoughts about Chad and his parents.

BRADLEY: Okay. One way that they baby him is not letting him go with me to. . . .

If your child remarks on your reflective listening, simply keep your cool and tell him that you are concerned about his feelings and thoughts. Don't let your child's reactions toward your reflective listening skills keep you from being a helpful parent.

## MAIN POINTS TO REMEMBER

- Reflective listening is summarizing and restating to your child, both her feelings and the situation causing those feelings.
- Use reflective listening to actively help your child understand and cope with her feelings.
- Reflective listening helps your child gain increased control over her emotions and behavior.

# 13
# More Problem Behavior—
# Questions and Solutions

In this chapter, we'll look at a variety of common child-hood problems: hyperactivity, specific learning disabilities, bedwetting, daytime enuresis, resisting chores, and bedtime problems. You'll learn more methods and skills for helping your child, including "racing the timer," "grounding," and the "resting chair." Also, you'll discover additional ways of using point rewards. Let's look at questions parents frequently ask.

**Q:** "My six-year-old son, Jeremy, is very active, always in motion, and doesn't pay attention when I tell him things. His first-grade teacher says that he is 'hyperactive' and has 'attention-deficit disorder.' How can I tell if Jeremy is hyperactive and, if so, what can I do to help him?"

**A:** A hyperactive child with attention-deficit disorder is persistently overactive, inattentive, and impulsive when compared with other children of the same age. Many hyperactive children experience learning problems at school, have difficulty getting along with peers, and are aggressive. Hyperactivity is about ten times more common in boys than in girls. Parents and teachers usually report feeling frustrated and worn out as they try to keep up with hyperactive children.

To determine whether Jeremy is hyperactive, have him examined by a pediatrician and evaluated by a psychologist. The psychologist probably will want to talk with Jeremy's teacher as well. Be consistent in applying the methods of child management described in this book. It's particularly important to give your child lots of praise for completing an activity or chore. Your pediatrician and psychologist will give you additional recommendations if they feel that Jeremy needs special help.

**Q:** "My six-year-old daughter dawdles when straightening her room, dressing for school, and going to bed. Is there any way I can help her speed up?"

**A:** To speed up your daughter's slow behavior, try an effective method called "racing the timer." Set a kitchen timer for a short period and reward her if she completes a task before the timer rings. For example, the next time you announce it's bedtime, set a timer for thirty or forty minutes. Tell her that she gets a bedtime story and a point on the point-reward calendar if she beats the timer. To beat the timer, she must finish her bedtime snack, put on her pajamas, brush her teeth, and be in bed when the timer rings.

Don't nag her to hurry and don't scold her if she loses the race. When she beats the timer, however, give her praise, a point on the calendar, and a bedtime story.

**Q:** "Are there more ways to use a timer to help my children?"

**A:** There are at least five ways to use a timer to improve behavior. Parents can time-out one child, two or more children, or toys that are involved in misbehavior. A timer can help children take turns when they want to play with the same toy, such as a video game. Also, as discussed previously, children can race the timer to speed up slow behavior. Timers are parent savers, because they are easy to use, effective in changing behavior, and save wear and tear on parents. Timers are also child savers, because they save children from having to listen to their parents nag and lecture them.

**Q:** "Occasionally, our twelve-year-old daughter gets in a bad mood, is grumpy, grouchy, complains about everything, criticizes her younger sister, and says annoying things to the rest of the family. Should I send her to her room for this unpleasant behavior?"

**A:** Yes, but first try reflective listening to determine what may be bothering her (see Chapter 12). Perhaps nothing specific is troubling your daughter; being grouchy with her family may just be a bad habit. Tell her that you understand that she feels grumpy. She has a right to her feelings, but she shouldn't subject the family to abusive behavior. Don't call it time-out, but send her to her room. Tell her that she may come out when she can stop grumbling, complaining, and criticizing her sister. Don't tell her how long to stay in her room; she decides when to come out. Fatigue sometimes causes grumpiness. If your daughter is grouchy because she is tired, she might decide to take a short nap before rejoining the family.

**Q:** "My seven- and ten-year-old children avoid helping my husband and me when we wash the car, rake leaves, or do dishes. They often say that they feel sick or tired or that they don't want to help. Are there any more methods to encourage children to help parents with work?"

**A:** A "resting chair" will encourage your child to help you with chores! This is the plan: Everyone who begins a chore works until it is completed—all the leaves are raked. If someone claims to feel sick or too tired to help the family, then that person must sit on the resting chair. The resting chair doesn't have to be an actual chair. If you are working outdoors, a spot under a particular tree will do fine. Be sure that the place is dull, boring, and free of interesting objects, but near another family member who is working. The person who is working serves as a good role model for the child who is resting!

A truly tired child—or adult—welcomes the opportunity to rest; however, if your child is pretending to be tired, he will soon get bored sitting in the resting chair and watching others. Most children will decide to leave the resting chair and help others with chores because they prefer some kind of activity to inactivity. Don't scold your child for sitting on the resting chair rather than working. Be sure that he doesn't get attention, play with toys, or leave the chair except to help others finish the job. A resting chair is boring, and boredom helps motivate children to work. After your children help with chores, be sure to tell them that you appreciate their hard work.

**Q:** "My nine-year-old son, Brandon, still wets the bed at night. I've heard that an alarm for bedwetting can help children to have dry nights. Could such an alarm help my son?"

**A:** Yes. Bedwetting alarms can help children six and older attain dry nights. Most children stop nighttime enuresis—wetting the bed—by the age of five or six. If they don't, they might need special help from their parents.

First, take Brandon to your pediatrician to be sure a medical problem isn't causing his bedwetting. Next, begin a special program to help Brandon. Follow these steps:

- Use a point-reward calendar as described in Chapter 10. The desired target behavior is dry nights, and Brandon should get a point for each night that he doesn't wet the bed. When he accumulates enough points, he selects a reward from a menu of rewards. Also, give him a lot of praise for each dry night. *Never scold or shame him for wetting the bed.* Undoubtedly, he already feels embarrassed or humiliated because of his problem.

- Whenever Brandon discovers that he wet the bed, he is to immediately shower or bathe and then place his wet sheets in the washer. This is a mild logical consequence for wetting his bed. Younger children need help from a parent in stripping a bed and drawing bath water. Steps one and two are often sufficient to help many children to completely stop wetting the bed within one or two months. However, if Brandon persists in bedwetting, continue with these two steps and begin step three.

- Order a bedwetting alarm from a mail-order catalog store such as Sears. The child sleeps on a special pad, which senses moisture and activates a battery-powered alarm. Since it takes only two seconds for the alarm to sound, Brandon will get instant feedback that he wet the bed. He will learn to correct his bedwetting by conditioning. He may need to use the alarm for a couple of months before he overcomes the problem. An alarm is extremely effective in helping children and adolescents to stop wetting the bed; however, if you purchase an alarm, also continue following the first two steps.

After attaining dry nights, your child may return to bedwetting. Don't despair. Simply follow the steps again. Most children don't return to bedwetting after a second time through the program; however, if your son or daughter needs additional help, you may wish to consult your pediatrician or a psychologist.

**Q:** "What help do you recommend for children who wet on themselves during the day, after they are toilet trained?"

**A:** A child who is five or older and toilet trained may slip back into occasional daytime enuresis. Try the following program:

Each day that your child is dry, give him three points on the point-reward calendar. If his problem is more frequent than once a day, divide the day into morning, afternoon, and evening. Give him a point for each part of the day that he is accident free. He can earn up to three points a day.

Encourage him to exchange his points for an item on the reward menu as soon as he earns enough points. Also, at the end of each day, compliment him if he hasn't had any accidents that day.

Never scold him for having an accident. Instead, have him immediately bathe, put on fresh clothes, and rinse out the soiled clothes himself.

**Q:** "My neighbors tell me that they restrict, or ground, their thirteen-year-old son for two or three weeks when he breaks rules. What is grounding, and do you recommend it as a method of discipline? I am thinking about using it with my teenage daughter."

**A:** *Grounding* is briefly restricting a child or adolescent to her home as a consequence for bad behavior. She isn't permitted to visit friends or to go places without her parents as she normally does. When used correctly, grounding can help preadolescents and teenagers to improve their behavior.

If you use grounding, be sure that you follow two rules. Tell your child in advance what misbehavior will cause grounding. Also, always keep the duration of grounding short—usually not more than a weekend or one week. Grounding a teenager for a period of two or three weeks is overly severe and is not an effective method for improving behavior.

**Q:** "My nine-year-old daughter, April, earns poor marks in school. Her teacher says that she may have a specific learning disability. What is a 'specific learning disability' and what should I do next in order to help my daughter?"

**A:** A specific learning disability means that a child's skill in reading, writing, or arithmetic is significantly below her age and intellectual capacity. Your daughter should be evaluated by a pediatrician and an eye doctor. It's also essential that you and your daughter talk to a psychologist and obtain measures of your child's intellectual capacity and educational skills. Be sure to follow the recommendations of the pediatrician and psychologist. A book by Osmon, described in Appendix B, gives parents suggestions for helping children with learning disabilities.

# MAIN POINTS TO REMEMBER

- This chapter gives you recommendations for common childhood problems such as hyperactivity, going to bed on time, resisting chores, bedwetting, daytime enuresis, and specific learning disabilities.
- Effective methods for helping children improve their behavior include racing the timer, sending a child to his room (not to time-out), the resting chair, grounding, and point rewards.
- Contact a pediatrician, psychologist, or family counselor for more help if the child management methods you're using aren't effective in helping your child.

# APPENDIXES
# MORE RESOURCES FOR HELPING YOUR CHILD

*You're not alone in the challenges of being a parent and assisting your son or daughter. Read this section and learn about various resources for parents.*

*Teachers spend many hours each week helping children. Appendix A tells how to work more effectively with your child's teacher. Appendix B gives information about joining parent education classes and about additional parenting books. Appendix C tells when and how to get professional help for your child or family. Appendix D provides tear-out reminder sheets for parents summarizing the main points discussed throughout the book.*

# Appendix A
# Teachers and Parents
# As Partners

In this appendix, you'll learn how to help improve your child's classroom work and personal adjustment by working effectively with his teacher.

Build a positive relationship with your child's teacher and demonstrate an interest in your child's school experiences by visiting the classroom. Quickly respond to notes from the teacher and school. Be the first to sign up to bring snacks and drinks for your son or daughter's class. Your child will appreciate the additional attention and interest in her classroom.

If you have time, consider volunteering to help the teacher. After first discussing it with your son or daughter, donate some of your time to your child's class. You might rearrange bulletin boards, organize bookshelves, or complete records.

Talk to your child about school. Children often bring their papers and completed projects home. Spend some time looking at your child's work. The best way for you to increase her good work is to reward it with attention and praise. Post your child's school papers on the refrigerator door for the whole family to admire.

Don't say negative things about the teacher in your child's presence. You want your child to respect the teacher. Also, remember that children frequently repeat things to their teacher that they hear at home.

Plan ahead if you want a productive parent-teacher conference. A *parent-teacher conference* is a face-to-face meeting between you and your child's teacher. As partners, you plan the best way to meet your child's educational and personal needs. What do you talk about at a conference? You might discuss your child's study habits, need for remedial work, or how to help her get along better with other children.

The school will probably contact you and schedule at least one or two conferences a year; however, you have the right to ask for additional conferences if your child needs special help. Don't be passive and wait for the teacher to contact you if your child is having difficulties. Don't assume if you hear nothing from the teacher that everything is fine, especially if your child has had school problems in the past.

Consider the following guidelines when contacting your child's teacher for a conference.

**Ask the teacher, at least a day in advance, to schedule a time to discuss your child's progress and adjustment.** Don't just "drop in" on the teacher and expect to have a productive conference. To talk to the teacher about a problem or to schedule a conference, call the school and ask that the teacher return your call.

**Make a list of things that you want to tell the teacher about your child and make a list of questions that you have about your child's progress.** Ask about your child's strongest and weakest subject areas and about any adjustment or behavior problems. If your spouse can't attend the conference, ask him or her for ideas when preparing your list.

**Don't bring your child to the conference unless the teacher specifically requests that you bring her.** Also, leave her brothers and sisters at home so that you and the teacher can devote full attention to discussing your child.

**During the conference, decide on specific plans to help your child.** Ask the teacher for suggestions and recommendations and honestly give these ideas a try. Agree on what the teacher is to do at school and what you are to do at home to help your child. Take notes concerning these future plans. Encourage the teacher to contact you if your child begins having problems at school.

**Be pleasant and nurture a positive working partnership between you and your child's teacher.** Tell the teacher that you appreciate the help that he or she is giving your child. If you feel that the teacher is doing a good job, let the teacher know it. Reward the teacher's "good behavior"!

Avoid getting upset and angry at the teacher and the school. Look for solutions to your child's problems, but avoid making the teacher feel responsible for those problems. Recognize that the teacher has at least twenty other children in the classroom. Understand the goals that the teacher and the school have for all children.

**Following your meeting with the teacher, share the results of the conference with your spouse and ask for help in following through with any suggestions and recommendations.** After the conference, tell your child about his strengths, problem areas needing improvement, and any plan of action decided upon by you and the teacher.

**Keep in close touch with your child's teacher.** Don't be afraid to ask for additional conferences. Teachers enjoy working with concerned parents who are strongly interested in their children. Teachers shouldn't mind additional conferences as long as you aren't blaming them for your child's problems.

If your child's teacher agrees, use a *parent-teacher-child record form* to improve your child's school work or behavior problems. Each day, the child takes the record form between home and school. The teacher indicates on the form whether or not a particular target behavior has occurred at school. When the child takes the record home, the parent can see if the target behavior occurred that day. The child then gains or loses a privilege at home that same afternoon or evening.

For example, seven-year-old John completed his morning seatwork only 62 percent of the time during a two-week period. He had the ability to do better, but he spent his time daydreaming and bothering children sitting near him. His teacher asked him and his parents to attend a joint conference where it was agreed to use the record form to help him.

Each day that John completed all of his morning seatwork, he earned the privilege of watching television at home between 3:00 P.M. and 5:00 P.M. that afternoon. If he failed to complete his seatwork or if he forgot the record form, then he couldn't watch television during those hours. John improved and instead of completing his seatwork only 62 percent of the time, he completed it 94 percent of the time! See the "Parent-Teacher-Child Record Form" used to help John.

Some record forms state that a privilege will be lost if a particular undesired target behavior such as fighting or teasing other children occurs. A record form provides your child, your child's teacher, and you with daily feedback regarding the progress of your child's target behavior. The record keeps everyone involved and coordinated in trying to improve the problem behavior. Since the record form requires extra time from

## PARENT-TEACHER-CHILD RECORD FORM—
## RECORD OF JOHN'S TARGET BEHAVIOR

Record of ___*John's*___ Target Behavior
(CHILD'S NAME)

Week of: ___*May 7th to 11th*___

Target behavior: ___*All*___
*morning seatwork completed; yes or no*
(TEACHER RECORDS EACH DAY)

| | M | T | W | T | F |
|---|---|---|---|---|---|
| (TEACHER RECORDS EACH DAY) | No | No | Yes | Yes | Yes |
| Teacher's initials: (TEACHER SIGNS EACH DAY) | CC | CC | CC | CC | CC |
| Child's initials: (CHILD SIGNS EACH DAY) | jb | jb | jb | jb | jb |
| Parent's initials: (PARENT SIGNS EACH DAY) | MB | MB | MB | MB | MB |

Plan: *If John completes all morning seatwork, he gets to watch television at home between 3:00 p.m. and 5:00 p.m. If seatwork is not completed or if John fails to bring this form home, then no television between 3:00 p.m. and 5:00 p.m.*

---

Each day John completes his seatwork at school, he gets the privilege of watching television at home that afternoon. For a copy of a parent-teacher-child record form, see the tear-out sheets in Appendix D.

the teacher, tell him or her that you appreciate the additional help.

When your child is upset about other children, the teacher, or classwork, use reflective listening to help her express her feelings and thoughts. Reflective listening skills are discussed in Chapter 12.

If your child has continuing difficulty with her schoolwork, you might consider obtaining a psychological evaluation of her educational skills, intellectual abilities, and level of motivation. The school might provide this evaluation. If not, you'll need to contact a psychologist yourself. Appendix C tells when and how to get professional help.

## MAIN POINTS TO REMEMBER

- Keep in close touch with the teacher to improve your child's behavior at school.
- Demonstrate an interest in your child's school experiences by visiting the classroom and by talking to her about school.

# Appendix B
# Useful Classes and Books for Parents

You'll want to continue learning additional parenting skills. This chapter tells how to join a parent education class or organize a parent study group. We'll also look at additional books which teach more parenting skills.

## JOINING PARENT EDUCATION CLASSES—WHAT TO EXPECT

Parent education classes are offered in most communities. The classes will provide you with increased knowledge and skills in helping your child. Usually six to twelve parents and a group leader meet for five to seven sessions, with each session lasting one or two hours.

Leaders of parent education classes teach by using tapes or films and by directing the group discussion. The group members learn principles of behavior and parenting strategies which are important in assisting all children, not just children with emotional or behavioral problems. These classes are not therapy sessions and the group leader won't attempt to diagnose or treat the problems of individual children.

Some parents who participate in parent education classes may have children who are experiencing significant emotional or behavioral problems. However, parent education classes usually deal with the normal challenges of rearing children faced by most parents.

Class leaders may follow the behavioral approach or they may use another orientation such as P.E.T. or STEP. You'll find that behavioral parent education classes are particularly consistent with *The Time-Out Solution.*

How do you find out about parent education classes in your community? These classes may be offered at child guidance clinics, adult education centers, mental health clinics, schools, churches, synagogues, community centers, and child development and psychology departments of universities. You may need to call several of these organizations in order to learn about the next classes scheduled in your community.

## FORMING YOUR OWN PARENT STUDY GROUP

Consider forming a small informal study group with other parents and discussing common problems of rearing children. Your discussions could center around a particular topic or child management book such as *The Time-Out Solution.* Parents whose children are about the same age often form a group. They have weekly meetings at each other's homes or at some place in the community. Toddlers can play while parents talk. However, normally it's more relaxing for parents to meet while their children are at preschool or elementary school.

To begin a parent study group, all you need are three or four parents who are interested in meeting together. You might consider organizing such a group yourself. In order for meetings to continue, a group member should agree to act as a coordinator or discussion leader for each succeeding meeting. Don't let one parent dominate the group discussion. Avoid discussing a son or daughter in front of that child or in the presence of other children.

# OTHER HELPFUL BOOKS FOR PARENTS

These practical books may be ordered from your local bookstore or the publisher.

## Parenting Books with a Behavioral Approach

Allen, J. *What Do I Do When?* San Luis Obispo, California: Impact Publishers, 1984.

The author presents methods for managing more than 50 common child-rearing problems.

Patterson, G. *Families: Applications of Social Learning to Family Life.* Champaign, Illinois: Research Press, 1975.

Basic principles of behavior are discussed. The author presents ways parents can help children who have a variety of problems. This parenting book is often recommended by behavioral family therapists.

Patterson, G., and Forgatch, M. *Parents and Adolescents Living Together.* Eugene, Oregon: Castalia Publishing Co., 1987.

The authors present effective methods that parents of teenagers can employ in order to improve family life.

## Parenting Books Without a Behavioral Approach

Dinkmeyer, D., and McKay, G. *The Parent's Handbook: Systematic Training for Effective Parenting.* Circle Pines, Minnesota: American Guidance Service, 1976.

This cartoon-illustrated book presents the child-rearing principles of the late Rudolf Dreikurs. The book emphasizes the use of natural and logical consequences, utilizes a family council approach to solving problems, and teaches parents how to help their children to express feelings. It is frequently used in parent education classes. A Spanish edition is available.

Dinkmeyer, D., and McKay, G. *The Parent's Guide: STEP/Teen: Systematic Training for Effective Parenting of Teens*. Circle Pines, Minnesota: American Guidance Service, 1983.

The orientation of this illustrated book is the same as the above book by Doctors Dinkmeyer and McKay. However, the book is for parents of teenagers.

Dreikurs, R., and Soltz, V. *Children: The Challenge*. New York: Hawthorne, 1964.

The orientation of this book is similar to the orientation of the books by Doctors Dinkmeyer and McKay described above.

Faber, A., and Mazlish, E. *How to Talk So Kids Will Listen and Listen So Kids Will Talk*. New York: Avon, 1980.

This illustrated book teaches effective communication skills to parents. The authors' orientation toward child rearing is influenced by the psychologist Haim Ginott, whose books are also listed below.

Ginott, H. *Between Parent and Child*. New York: Avon, 1965.

The author tells parents how to communicate with children and how to build mutual respect between parent and child.

Ginott, H. *Between Parent and Teenager*. New York: Avon, 1971.

This book has the same orientation as the above book, but is intended for parents of teenagers.

Gordon, T. *P.E.T.: Parent Effectiveness Training.* New York: Plume, 1970.

This approach to child rearing stresses communication skills for parents.

Osmon, B. *Learning Disabilities: A Family Affair.* New York: Random House, 1979.

This book gives realistic suggestions for helping children who are of normal intelligence but who have a learning disability.

Schaefer, C. *How to Talk to Children About Really Important Things.* New York: Harper & Row, 1984.

The author tells parents how to talk to children about thirty-six really important but sensitive issues such as sex, death, religion, and going to the doctor.

## MAIN POINTS TO REMEMBER

- Consider taking a parent education class.
- Think about organizing your own parent study group.
- Learn additional parenting skills by reading one of the previously mentioned books.

# Appendix C
# When and How to Get Professional Help

Raising your child from infancy through adolescence is a long and sometimes difficult journey. Problems can arise and interfere with your family's well-being and happiness. If difficulties persist in spite of your best efforts to resolve them, avoid giving in to hopelessness, guilt, depression, or anger. Contact a counselor or therapist for professional help. Consider the following questions and suggestions when thinking about counseling for your child or family.

**Q:** "When should I get professional help for my child?"

**A:** As a parent, it's your responsibility to help your child and family to understand and solve problems. Consider getting professional help if your child is persistently unhappy or has significant difficulty in adjusting to school, peers, or other family members. Professional help may also be needed if your child is causing you or other family members a lot of distress. You may feel that your usual methods of managing your child aren't working or that your child's behavior is beyond control. If your child becomes violent when disciplined or won't cooperate with the time-out method, then you and your child may need some direct help from a professional counselor.

**Q:** "How do I learn about professional counseling services in my area?"

**A:** It often requires a lot of effort to learn about competent counselors and appropriate helping agencies in your community. Most pediatricians and family physicians can advise you about local family therapists and counselors. Ask your physician to recommend the names of at least two counselors. Some physicians may prematurely reassure worried parents with, "Your child is just going through a stage" or, "He'll outgrow all those problems." Consider what your physician says, but also discuss the indications and benefits of counseling with one of the counselors.

When contacting your pediatrician or physician, you may wish to discuss the possibility of a complete physical examination for your child before counseling begins. If your pediatrician suggests drugs to help control your child's behavior, you might consider getting a second opinion from another pediatrician.

Other sources of information about counselors or appropriate agencies include school principals and counselors, teachers, the clergy, and friends. Most telephone crisis lines and community mental health centers are also valuable sources of information about available counseling services. Telephone directories list psychiatrists, psychologists, marriage and family counselors, and clinical social workers.

If your child has a learning problem at school, he should be seen by a qualified psychologist for an evaluation that includes psychological testing. Most school systems provide a psychological evaluation with recommendations if a child is experiencing learning or behavior problems at school; however, the thoroughness of psychological evaluations provided by schools is quite variable. Also, schools don't provide parent-child counseling services.

Professionals who offer therapy and counseling to children and adults include psychiatrists (M.D.), psychologists (Ph.D., Psy.D., M.A., or M.S.), marriage and family counselors (Ph.D., M.A., or M.S.), and clinical social workers (M.S.W.). They usually belong to one or more of the following organizations.

American Association for Marriage and Family
 Therapy (AAMFT)
1717 K Street, N.W., Suite 407
Washington, D.C. 20026

American Psychiatric Association (APA)
1700 18th Street, N.W.
Washington, D.C. 20009

American Psychological Association (APA)
1200 17th Street, N.W.
Washington, D.C. 20036

Association for Advancement of Behavior
 Therapy (AABT)
15 West 36th Street
New York, NY 10018

Association for Behavior Analysis (ABA)
Department of Psychology
Western Michigan University
Kalamazoo, MI 49008

National Association of Social Workers (NASW)
7981 Eastern Avenue
Silver Spring, MD 20910

National Register of Health Service Providers
  in Psychology
1200 Seventeenth Street, N.W.
Washington, D.C. 20036
(Psychologists who apply for and meet specified
  standards of training and experience are listed in
  this national register.)

**Q:** "What do I ask the family counselor during our first contact?"

**A:** After obtaining the names of a couple of counselors or counseling agencies, you will need to telephone a counselor or agency. If the counselor is in private-independent practice, make a list of questions, and ask to speak directly with the counselor. Briefly, tell the counselor the nature of your child's difficulties. Ask if he helps children with such difficulties. If not, ask whom he or she would recommend to help you and your child. Inquire about the training, experience, and certification he has for working with children and families. Ask about the cost of each visit, how many visits will probably be necessary, and over what period of time. When first beginning therapy and counseling, weekly visits are important.

**Q:** "How do I tell my child that we are going to see a family counselor?"

**A:** Use direct, simple language when telling your child that the family or the two of you are going to meet with a counselor. Be positive and tell your child that the counselor will help to solve problems. For example, you might say, "Everyone in our family has been arguing a lot the last few months. We have an appointment with a counselor who will help us to understand our problems and to get along better."

If your child has been receiving low grades in school, you might say, "We're going to meet with a psychologist. She'll give you some tests, talk to you, and talk to me also. She'll offer us some ideas about how to help you with your schoolwork and grades. We have an appointment Wednesday afternoon."

**Q:** "What should I expect when we begin counseling?"

**A:** The first couple of sessions will focus on evaluation and assessment. The counselor will help evaluate and clarify the problems confronting you and your family. Since your spouse is a central part of the family, he or she should also become involved in counseling. In addition to talking with you about your child's difficulties, the counselor will ask about the expectations and goals that you have as a parent. You'll fill out brief questionnaires and keep records of your child's behavior. The counselor will talk with your child and observe you and your child together.

After evaluating the problems troubling you and your child, the counselor will help you to solve these difficulties. Depending upon the problems to be resolved, counselors may use one or more possible approaches.

## FOUR APPROACHES TO HELPING CHILDREN AND PARENTS

• The counselor does therapy directly with your child. Most parents probably expect this treatment method, although this approach by itself is limited in its effectiveness.

- The counselor teaches you new methods for helping and managing your child. You also may be asked to read parenting materials (perhaps this book!).
- The counselor helps you to understand and resolve your own personal problems. Such problems often include depression, life crises, or marital difficulties.
- The counselor meets with your entire family in counseling sessions. Some problems are best treated by working with the whole family, at one time.

Be willing to modify your expectations for counseling and be flexible in working with your counselor. However, always ask your counselor any questions that you may have about counseling. With your permission, the counselor may contact your child's teacher and recommend additional ways the school can help your child.

**Q:** "How do I pay for professional services?"

**A:** Counseling costs money, but so do health care, education, transportation, family entertainment, going out to eat, and vacations. Counseling can help to reduce your child's behavioral and emotional problems and to increase his personal competence and social skills. It can improve the quality of family life.

Counselors in private-independent practice usually have a set fee for each counseling session. Community mental health agencies, however, usually charge on a sliding scale based on family income. To determine if your medical insurance might cover all or part of your expenses, check with your insurance company and talk with the counselor. If a public school system is providing psychological testing and evaluation, there won't be a charge. Your taxes pay for these services!

# MAIN POINTS TO REMEMBER

- Family and behavior problems sometimes become difficult for parents to handle.
- Counselors can help you and your family to resolve problems.
- Consider getting professional help if your usual methods of managing your child or handling family problems aren't working.

# Appendix D
# Tear-Out Reminder Sheets
# for Parents

# BASIC CHILD-REARING RULES AND ERRORS

What can you do to help improve his or her behavior? Follow three basic child-rearing rules and avoid four possible errors. These rules and errors are discussed in Chapter 1.

---

### THREE CHILD-REARING RULES

**Rule 1.** Reward good behavior (and do it quickly and often).

**Rule 2.** Don't "accidentally" reward bad behavior.

**Rule 3.** Punish some bad behavior (but use mild punishment only).

---

### FOUR CHILD-REARING ERRORS TO AVOID

**Error 1.** Parents fail to reward good behavior.

**Error 2.** Parents "accidentally" punish good behavior.

**Error 3.** Parents "accidentally" reward bad behavior.

**Error 4.** Parents fail to punish bad behavior (when mild punishment is indicated).

# REWARDS CHILDREN LIKE

It's important to reward your child's good behavior. Rewarding good behavior is the easiest and best way to improve behavior. What rewards should parents use? Rewards that motivate children are social rewards, activity rewards, and material rewards.

| REWARDS CHILDREN LIKE | | |
|---|---|---|
| Social Rewards | Activity Rewards, Including Privileges | Material Rewards |
| Smiles | Play cards with parent | Ice-cream |
| Hugs | Go to park | Ball |
| Pats | Look at book with | Money |
| Attention | parent | Book |
| Touching | Help bake cookies | Jump rope |
| Clapping | Watch a late TV movie | Balloons |
| hands | Have a friend over | Yo-yo |
| Winks | Play ball with parent | Flashlight |
| Praise | Play a game together | Special |
| "Good job" | Go out for pizza | dessert |
| "Well done" | together | Record |

It's also important to fail to reward your child's bad behavior. If you accidentally reward bad behavior, you will strengthen that bad behavior.

Reward only good behavior and do it quickly and often. Basic child-rearing rules and common errors are discussed in Chapter 1.

# HOW TO GIVE EFFECTIVE INSTRUCTIONS AND COMMANDS TO YOUR CHILD

You must be able to give clear, effective instructions and commands on occasion. You must also be able to "back up" your commands. A command is a request to immediately start or stop a behavior.

When are commands given? Give your child a command when you want him to stop a specific misbehavior and you believe that he might disobey a simple request to stop the misbehavior. Also, give a command when you want your child to start a particular behavior and you believe that your child might disobey a simple request to start the behavior.

How should you give a command? Follow the guidelines listed below:

---

### GIVING EFFECTIVE COMMANDS TO YOUR CHILD

**Steps to follow:**

• Move close to your child.

• Have a stern facial expression.

• Say his or her name.

• Get and maintain eye contact.

• Use a firm tone of voice.

• Give a direct, simple, and clear command.

• "Back up" your command, if necessary.

---

# BASIC STEPS FOR INITIALLY USING
# TIME-OUT—PARENTS' CHECKLIST

✓

_____    **Steps to follow:**

_____    1. Select one target behavior for which
              to use time-out.

_____    2. Count how often this target behavior
              occurs.*

_____    3. Pick out a boring place for time-out.

_____    4. Explain time-out to your child.

_____    5. Wait patiently for the target behavior
              to occur.

### TARGET BEHAVIOR OCCURS!

_____    6. Place your child in the time-out place
              and use no more than ten words and
              ten seconds.

_____    7. Get the portable timer, set it to ring
              one minute for each year of your
              child's age, and place it within hearing
              distance of your child.

_____    8. Wait for the timer to ring—remove all
              attention from your child while he or
              she waits for the timer to ring.

_____    9. Ask your child, after the timer rings,
              why he or she was sent to time-out.

---

*This step is important but not essential.

## METHODS OF MILD PUNISHMENT—COMPARISON FOR PARENTS

| Method of Mild Punishment | Age of Child | Effectiveness of Punishment | Type of Behavior Punished | How Quickly Applied |
|---|---|---|---|---|
| Time-Out | Two through twelve years | Extremely effective | Most behavior, especially hard-to-handle behavior | Immediately, if possible |
| Scolding and Disapproval | All ages | Moderately effective | All behavior | Immediately or later |
| Natural Consequences | All ages | Effective | Some behavior | Immediately or later |
| Logical Consequences | Three through adolescence | Effective | Most behavior | Immediately or later |
| Behavior Penalty | Five through adolescence | Effective | All behavior | Immediately or later |

| POINT-REWARD CALENDAR FOR IMPROVING SEVERAL BEHAVIORS | | | | | | | |
|---|---|---|---|---|---|---|---|
| **Points Earned** | | | | | | | |
| **List of Good Behavior (and possible points)** | **S** | **M** | **T** | **W** | **T** | **F** | **S** |
| | | | | | | | |
| | | | | | | | |
| | | | | | | | |
| | | | | | | | |
| | | | | | | | |
| | | | | | | | |
| **Total Points Earned** | | | | | | | |

This calendar provides a record of several kinds of behavior for one week. Post a new calendar each week.

At the end of each day, total the number of points your child has earned. Draw marks through points on the bottom line when your child spends those points. Chapter 10 describes how to use a point-reward calendar to improve your child's behavior.

| MENU OF REWARDS | |
|---|---|
| **Reward** | **Cost in Points** |
| | |

List material rewards and activity rewards on this menu. Also list the number of points (or tokens) that your child must pay for each reward. Post this menu next to the point-reward calendar.

Chapter 10 describes how to use a menu of rewards to improve your child's behavior.

## PARENT-CHILD CONTRACT FORM

### Contract

I, _____ , agree to: _____
(CHILD'S NAME)

_____

_____

_____

_____

We, Mother and Father, agree to: _____

_____

_____

_____

Date contract begins:   _____

Date contract ends:   _____

Date contract signed:   _____

Agreed to by:   _____
(CHILD'S SIGNATURE)

_____
(MOTHER)

_____
(FATHER)

Chapter 10 describes how to use parent-child contracts.

## PARENT-TEACHER-CHILD RECORD FORM

Record of _____ Target Behavior
(CHILD'S NAME)

Week of: _____

Target behavior: _____

| | M | T | W | T | F |
|---|---|---|---|---|---|
| (TEACHER RECORDS EACH DAY) | | | | | |
| Teacher's initials: (TEACHER SIGNS EACH DAY) | | | | | |
| Child's initials: (CHILD SIGNS EACH DAY) | | | | | |
| Parent's initials: (PARENT SIGNS EACH DAY) | | | | | |

Plan: _____

_____

_____

_____

Appendix A describes how to use parent-teacher-child record forms.

# References

Alberto, P. A., and Troutman, A. C. *Applied Behavior Analysis for Teachers.* Columbus, OH: Charles Merrill Publishing Company, 1982.

Allen, J. *What Do I Do When?* San Luis Obispo, CA: Impact Publishers, 1984.

American Psychiatric Association. *Diagnostic and Statistical Manual of Mental Disorders, Third Edition, Revised.* Washington, DC: American Psychiatric Association, 1987.

Bandura, A., and Walters, R. H. *Social Learning and Personality Development.* New York: Holt, Rinehart & Winston, 1963.

Barkley, R. A. *Hyperactive Children: A Handbook for Diagnosis and Treatment.* New York: Guilford Press, 1981.

Becker, W. C. *Parents are Teachers: A Child Management Program.* Champaign, IL: Research Press, 1971.

Bernal, M. E. "Consumer Issues in Parent Training." In R. F. Dangel and R. A. Polster (eds.), *Parent Training:*

*Foundations of Research and Practice* (477–546). New York: Guilford Press, 1984.

Bernal, M. E., and North, J. A. "A Survey of Parent Training Manuals." *Journal of Applied Behavior Analysis* (11: 533–544), 1978.

Blackham, G. J., and Silberman, A. *Modification of Child and Adolescent Behavior* (3rd ed.). Belmont, CA: Wadsworth Publishing Co., 1980.

Bureau of Education for Exceptional Children, Kentucky Department of Education. *A.B.C's of a Parent-Teacher Conference.* Frankfort, KY: Author, 1971.

Christophersen, E. R. *Little People* (2nd ed.). Lawrence, KS: H&H Enterprises, 1982.

Clark, L. F. *Time Out and 10-10-10.* Unpublished manuscript, 1972.

Dangel, R. F., and Polster, R. A. "Winning! A Systematic, Empirical Approach to Parent Training." In R. F. Dangel and R. A. Polster (eds.), *Parent Training: Foundations of Research and Practice* (162–201). New York: Guilford Press, 1984.

Dangel, R. F., and Polster, R. A. *Teaching Child Management Skills.* New York: Pergamon Press, 1988.

DeRisi, W. J., and Butz, G. *Writing Behavioral Contracts: A Case Simulation Practice Manual.* Champaign, IL: Research Press, 1975.

Dinkmeyer, D., and McKay, G. *The Parent's Handbook: Systematic Training for Effective Parenting.* Circle Pines, MN: American Guidance Service, 1976.

Dinkmeyer, D., and McKay, G. *The Parent's Guide: STEP/Teen.* Circle Pines, MN: American Guidance Service, 1983.

Dreikurs, R., and Grey, L. *A Parents' Guide to Child Discipline.* New York: Hawthorn Books, 1968.

Dreikurs, R., and Soltz, V. *Children: The Challenge.* New York: Hawthorn, 1964.

Egan, G. *The Skilled Helper: Models, Skills, and Methods for Effective Helping* (2nd ed.). Monterey, CA: Brooks/Cole Publishing Company, 1982.

Eimers, R., and Aitchison, R. *Effective Parents/Responsible Children.* New York: McGraw-Hill Book Co., 1977.

Faber, A., and Mazlish, E. *How to Talk So Kids Will Listen and Listen So Kids Will Talk.* New York: Avon, 1980.

Forehand, R. L., and King, E. "Pre-school children's noncompliance: Effects of short-term behavior therapy." *Journal of Community Psychology* (2: 42–44), 1974.

Forehand, R. L., and McMahon, R. J. *Helping the Noncompliant Child.* New York: Guilford Press, 1981.

Gast, D. L., and Nelson, C. M. "Legal and Ethical Considerations for the Use of Timeout in Special Education Settings." *Journal of Special Education* (11: 457–467), 1977.

Gelfand, D. M., and Hartman, D. P. *Child Behavior Analysis and Therapy* (2nd ed.). New York: Pergamon Press, 1984.

Ginott, H. *Between Parent and Child.* New York: Avon, 1965.

Ginott, H. *Between Parent and Teenager.* New York: Avon, 1971.

Gordon, T. *P.E.T.: Parent Effectiveness Training.* New York: Plume, 1970.

Hall, R. V., and Hall, M. C. *How to Use Time Out.* Lawrence, KS: H&H Enterprises, 1980.

Hall, R. V., and Hall, M. C. *How to Negotiate a Behavioral Contract.* Lawrence, KS: H&H Enterprises, 1982.

Hobbs, S. A., and Forehand, R. "Important Parameters in the Use of Time out with Children: A Re-examination." *Journal of Behavior Therapy and Experimental Psychiatry* (8: 365–370), 1977.

Hobbs, S. A., Forehand, R., and Murray, R. G. "Effects of Various Durations of Time out on the Noncompliant Behavior of Children." *Behavior Therapy* (9: 652–659), 1978.

Lindsley, O. R. "An Experiment with Parents Handling Behavior at Home." *Johnstone Bulletin* (9: 27–36), 1966.

Madsen, C. H., and Madsen, C. K. *Teaching/Discipline: A Positive Approach for Educational Development* (3rd ed.). Boston: Allyn and Bacon, 1981.

Martin, G., and Pear, J. *Behavior Modification: What It Is and How to Do It*. Englewood Cliffs, NJ: Prentice-Hall, Inc., 1983.

Mason, D. "How to Grow a Parents' Group." *Parents* (60: 194–200), 1983.

Matson, J. L., and Dilorenzo, T. M. *Punishment and Its Alternatives: A New Perspective for Behavior Modification*. New York: Springer Publishing Co., 1984.

Nolan, P. Personal communication, Dec. 1984.

Osmon, B. *Learning Disabilities: A Family Affair*. New York: Random House, 1979.

Patterson, G. R. *Families: Applications of Social Learning to Family Life*. Champaign, IL: Research Press, 1975.

Patterson, G. R. "The Aggressive Child: Victim and Architect of a Coercive System." In E. J. Mash, L. A. Hamerlynck and L. C. Handy (eds.), *Behavior Modification and Families* (267–316). New York: Brunner/Mazel, 1976.

Patterson, G. R. *A Social Learning Approach*. Vol. 3: *Coercive Family Process*. Eugene, OR: Castalia Publishing Co., 1982.

Patterson, G. R. "Prevention of Antisocial Behavior: A Problem in Three Levels." Paper presented at the meeting of Association for Advancement of Behavior Therapy, Philadelphia, PA, Nov. 1984. The term *nattering* was coined by J. Reid.

Patterson, G. R., and Forgatch, M. (Producers). *Family Living Series: Part I* (audiocassette program no. 0026). Champaign, IL: Research Press, 1975.

Patterson, G. R., and Forgatch, M. *Parents and Adolescents Living Together.* Eugene, OR: Castalia Publishing Co., 1987.

Polster, R. A., and Dangel, R. F. (eds.). *Parent Training: Foundations of Research and Practice.* New York: Guilford Press, 1984.

Premack, D. "Toward Empirical Behavior Laws: 1. Positive Reinforcement." *Psychological Review* (66: 219–233), 1959.

Roberts, M. W. "Parent Handouts 1,2,3," 1982. (Available from Mark Roberts, Idaho State University, Pocatello, ID.)

Roberts, M. W. "Resistance to Time out: Some Normative Data." *Behavioral Assessment* (4: 237–246), 1982.

Roberts, M. W. Personal communication, Dec. 28, 1984.

Roberts, M. W., McMahon, R. J., Forehand, R., and Humphreys, L. "The Effect of Parental Instruction-Giving on Child Compliance." *Behavior Therapy* (9: 793–798), 1978.

Schaefer, C. E. *Childhood Encopresis and Enuresis: Causes and Therapy.* New York: Van Nostrand Reinhold, 1979.

Schaefer, C. E. *How to Talk to Children About Really Important Things.* New York: Harper & Row, 1984.

Skinner, B. F. *Science and Human Behavior.* New York: Macmillan, 1953.

Sulzer-Azaroff, B., and Mayer, G. R. *Applying Behavior-Analysis Procedures with Children and Youth.* New York: Holt, Rinehart and Winston, 1977.

Wagonseller, B. R., Burnett, M., Salzberg, B., and Burnett, J. *The Art of Parenting Kit: A Complete Training Kit* (filmstrip and audiocassette kit no. 1810). Champaign, IL: Research Press, 1977.

Wilson, G. T., and O'Leary, K. D. *Principles of Behavior Therapy.* Englewood Cliffs, NJ: Prentice-Hall, Inc., 1980.

Wright, L. *Parent Power: A Guide to Responsible Child-Rearing.* New York: Psychological Dimensions, Inc., 1978.

# Index